Worldchanging 101

Challenging the Myth of Powerlessness

David LaMotte

Edited by Virginia Bairby

© 2014 Dryad Publishing, Inc.
P.O. Box 551
Montreat, NC 28757

ISBN: 978-0-9906500-0-3
LCCN: 2014913706

Edited by Virginia Bairby.

Layout and design by Kudzu Branding Company
www.kudzubranding.com

Printed in Canada, by Friesens Printing.
www.friesens.com

10 9 8 7 6 5 4 3 2 1

ENVIRONMENTAL BENEFITS STATEMENT

David LaMotte saved the following resources by printing the pages of this book on chlorine free paper made with 100% post-consumer waste.

TREES	WATER	ENERGY	SOLID WASTE	GREENHOUSE GASES
23	**10,894**	**11**	**729**	**2,009**
FULLY GROWN	GALLONS	MILLION BTUs	POUNDS	POUNDS

Environmental impact estimates were made using the Environmental Paper Network Paper Calculator 3.2. For more information visit www.papercalculator.org.

Contents

For Deanna and Mason, who have changed
my world and enriched my life
more than I could have imagined.

You are my home.

Acknowledgements

I have been working on writing this book for several years now, and, as with all good efforts to have a positive impact, there have been many people involved who need to be thanked. I'm sure I will only remember to list some of them here, but I hope that friends whom I omit will understand my gratitude through other means.

I need to thank the author Paul Loeb profusely. A portion of this book is simply an account of my own wrestling and experimentation with ideas I first encountered in his books *Soul of a Citizen* and *The Impossible Will Take a Little While*. If the ideas in this book are interesting to you, I highly recommend that you read everything he has written.

My wife Deanna is a wise voice in my life, as well as being my true love, and I'm grateful to her for making me actually finish this (pursuant to a rule she established for me: I can't start the next big project until I finish the current one). I'm so deeply grateful to her for believing in the value of this effort and actively making space for it, not to mention for marrying me, being such a wonderful wife and mother, and weaving her life together with mine.

Ginna Bairby has been an extraordinary editor, generously offering her skills with words, sentences, paragraphs, chapters, and the trajectory of a whole book—and being extremely patient with my over-committed, deadline-missing self.

Eric Jackson is both my brother-in-law and my manager, and I'm deeply grateful to be wrangled and guided by him. He's making my life work better in all sorts of ways, and I'm thrilled that he's my colleague as well as a part of my family.

My friends Caroline and Allen made their lovely mountain retreat available to me for a week-long silent writer's retreat that made space for significant progress on this effort. I could not be more grateful.

Tamara Feightner and Barbie Angell do a wonderful job running my office and handling my booking, working as hard as they can to give me space to write. They are also my friends, and

I'm deeply grateful for those good gifts.

Josh Richard has been extraordinarily generous with his time and creative talent on this and several other projects I've taken on.

First readers for the book include some family, some close friends, and some people with deep life experience in the work of changing the world (often in overlapping categories). Deep gratitude to Dennis Smith, Mindy Maddux, Liz Frencham, Hugh Hollowell, Rob Stephens, Will Nash, Jamie and Gwyn Ridenhour, my wife Deanna, my sister Kathy LaMotte, and my parents John and Olivia LaMotte. Margaret Aymer Oget and Deb Fox helped me think through some thorny questions of wording and wisdom, and Brian O'Connors, Maryl Neff, Ed Loring, Patrick Miller, and David Gill helped to correct some of my faulty recollections, and I'm sincerely grateful for that. Their feedback has been tremendously valuable.

I had lunch with Eric Bannan a couple of years ago and told him about the book. He gave me great feedback on the title, in particular. Thanks, Eric.

Murphy, Kenny, Jeff, and Max at Kudzu Branding and Design Co. have been a great team on this project, including the book design, and are great friends and neighbors, too. Peter Councell at Be Heard Media has been instrumental in getting the word out, and Chris Liu-Beers is a great guru in the realm of all things website related.

One of the main themes of this book is discernment, trying to perceive the path in front of us. I am deeply grateful to Friends at Swannanoa Valley Friends Meeting for providing the space to listen for leading, and deep, sustaining friendship. I look to my faith community to challenge me and nourish me in equal measure, and I find both gifts there.

Sincere thanks to friends at the Montreat Conference Center, which has been a connecting point for so many people and experiences that I treasure. Thanks for continuing to invite me back after all these years and for serving the world in all the ways that you do.

Thanks to my colleagues on the AFSC Nobel Peace Prize Nominating Task Group, past and present. I have learned so much from you, and I am sure I will continue to. Thank you for your peaceful presence and diligent work in seeking peace and pursuing it, not to mention your patience with my learning curve.

Special thanks to George Reed and the staff at the North Carolina Council of Churches for their confidence, friendship, and mentoring. My journey is so much richer for my time there.

Special thanks as well to Rotary International and the Rotary Foundation for select-ing me as a Rotary World Peace Fellow. That opportunity and experience have opened doors and enriched my life in ways that I could never have imagined, and I am grateful to you for believing in my capacity to change the world, as well as for the changes you are effecting yourselves.

I love the fact that the funding for this book mirrors one of its messages—that through the accumulation of many efforts, small and large, we can do so much more than we can do on our own.

Most of the costs of the initial printing of this book were covered through Kickstarter.com, where 357 funders contributed a total of over $20,000 to make it happen. I am deeply grateful to everyone who helped birth this book by joining that effort, with special thanks to Sherri Powers, Rick and Jackie Holcombe, Lisa Silverstein Tzur, and the Rotary Club of Brisbane Planetarium in Brisbane, Australia. I love the fact that the funding for this book mirrors one of its messages—that through the accumulation of many efforts, small and large, we can do so much more than we can do on our own. I should also acknowledge that each of those funders chose to back the book before they had a chance to read it, believing in me and my work enough to trust that this would be a good thing. That means that they may not agree with everything I say here.

Lastly, and most importantly, thanks to *you* for reading this book. Doing so is an indication that you care; you know that your world has a population of more than one. Human beings make the most sense in community, and community can only be created by risking, by reaching past the places where we are comfortable. I hope this book will both encourage and challenge you. Regardless of how you intersect with it, though, thank you for being the kind of person who would read such a book. Blessings on your efforts to change the world for the better.

Preface

Srikakulam, Andhra Pradesh, India
November 5, 2009

As I write these words, I am sitting on the second floor of a cement water tower that has had two guest rooms built into it just below the tank, one of which I'll be using as a bit of office space for the next couple of months. This unusual building is in the small village of Srikakulam, in the southern state of Andhra Pradesh, India. If I climb a couple more flights of stairs up to the roof, I can look out at people working in the fields below, cutting and stacking hay to feed the water buffalo that graze just outside my door. Milk from one of those buffalo was in my tea this morning.

I am here to work with an Indian non-profit community development organization, Arthik Samata Mandal, doing field work for my masters degree. The organization is run by the descendants of a legendary Gandhian activist who went by the name of Gora. Most of his nine children remain actively involved in social justice and sustainable development work, and the next generation contains some impressive peace and justice workers as well.

It is an extraordinary opportunity.

My experience in India so far has been gritty, intense, and discouraging, while at the same time overflowing with kindness, warmth, and hope. Those things are not mutually exclusive. They may be mixed together in a single day as inextricably as the buffalo milk in my chai.

My wife, my one-year-old, and I bathe with a small bucket and a mug, and we use the same bucket to wash our clothes. We have learned to eat with our hands; by now it's somewhat natural and reasonably effective. Toilet paper is not common here. These things are not really hardships; to be honest, this is more or less how the vast majority of the world lives. Still, they are unfamiliar to us and serve as daily reminders of our usual privilege, and of the fact that there are many different definitions of 'normal'.

They are also reminders of the personal cost of middle class material comfort and its tendency to remove us from our own surroundings. In India, Haiti, Guatemala, and other 'developing countries' where I've been fortunate enough to eat and sleep from time to time, I find that death seems a little closer. It is not kept out of sight so that we can deny its reality; it is a present possibility in each new day (certainly any day that involves driving in Indian traffic!).

The beautiful and surprising corollary is that *life* seems closer as well. The colors are somehow more vivid, the tastes richer on my tongue, the relationships and casual interactions are somehow less disposable.

Last Sunday afternoon, I spent a few hours talking with Lavanam, the second oldest of the Gora children. Eighty years old as of this writing, Lavanam is still politically active on various issues, including the ongoing negotiations between the Indian government and the Naxalite Maoist rebels in the hills nearby. He has been in dialogue with the rebels in recent years, arguing for the value of non-violence as a tool in their often violent revolutionary struggle; at the same time, he's been meeting with the government regarding the legitimacy of the rebels' concerns about the marginalization of the rural poor. Though he has written many books, Lavanam is no ivory tower academic, distant from the gritty realities of conflict and poverty.

Lavanam also told me stories of his teenage years and conversations he had with Gandhi while living on his ashram, as well as his many decades of passionate engagement since then. As we talked, he articulated one of his central concerns about development work: that most international development work is based on a Western model and is, therefore, *opportunity*-based.

Creating opportunities is not a bad thing in and of itself, but Lavanam argues that opportunity-based development, in the sense that he is using the term, can be destructive to community because it appeals primarily to individualist and materialist motivations. What is needed, he argues, is *value*-based development, which does not ask how an individual may better his or her lot, but rather asks how an individual may contribute to the betterment of his or her community.

I am still early in my time here, and I know there are many stories to come. I love good stories, whether I'm the one listening to them or telling them, and that may be why I have been invited to speak to various groups in recent years about some of my experiences.

In those talks, I often frame my thoughts around ideas of how we as individuals can have a positive impact on the world around us, what could be called 'practical idealism'. I am a firm believer that the vast majority of people on the planet have much more potential to change the world than we give ourselves credit for. The main thing standing in the way for most of us is a belief in limitations that don't actually exist.

What is needed, he argues, is value-based development, which does not ask how an individual may better his or her lot, but rather asks how an individual may contribute to the betterment of his or her community.

Let me clarify, however, that while I am unashamedly interested in motivating people, my workshops bear little resemblance to 'motivational speaking' as it is currently understood, which generally means motivating people for personal gain and enrichment. That holds little interest or appeal for me. I am much more interested in Lavanam's value-based context for the conversation—motivating people to have a positive impact on their larger social contexts, not just on their individual material situations. I think that serves everyone better, and there is research to back that conclusion up.

In their book *The Dragonfly Effect*, Andy Smith and Jennifer Lynn Aaker cite a sociological study that examined both people's perceptions of what makes them happy and what *really* does. What they found was that people tend to believe that material gain, affluence, and leisure make them happy (a job promotion, a new car, a trip to the Bahamas, etc.).

When they interviewed people who consider themselves happy, however, those factors were not significantly correlated. Rather, they found that the common denominator among people who really *are* happy is a sense that their lives are meaningful. That they matter. That they are of service.

That rings true to me, and it is one reason I'm writing this book. At its core, this book is about practical ways to live a life that matters and some of the stories we tell that impede our doing so.

This book bears a title that my Aussie friends might describe as 'cheeky': *Worldchanging 101*. A title like that might seem to suggest that I have the answers as to how to change the world, and I will hereby proceed to share them with you. This is, of course, not the case.

> The commmom denommimator among people who really are happy is a sense that their lives are meanimgful.

I would argue, though, that any *good* first year university course (which we often call a '101' course in the United States), doesn't actually offer answers, but instead reframes the questions and asks students to think about them in new ways. I sincerely hope you will test the ideas I offer here against your own practical knowledge and reject the ones that don't square with your experience with as much enthusiasm as you celebrate the ones which may ring true. Discerning what we *don't* believe is as fundamental to our growth and education as discovering what we *do* believe, and if these words serve that purpose for you, I can only celebrate that.

I have also come to believe that the stories we tell, sharing our own experiences and the experiences of others who have had an impact on us, matter a great deal. Having valued others' stories deeply, it seems right to offer a few of my own, in the hope that they may be helpful to you.

I don't claim any impressive scholarship on these topics or long lists of direct action campaigns in social change movements, though I've had some experience in each area, and I expect the years to come will offer further opportunities for both.

Even if I had those credentials, though, I would not want that to add any more weight to what I am offering here. My hope is that you will consider the *ideas* in their own inherent value. It doesn't really matter who is offering them.

I think the most credibility I can honestly claim is that I am the internationally recognized world's leading authority on my own experience. As I have lived through what is likely at least half of my life story, I have wrestled with my own sense of call and capacity for impact, both intellectually and practically, by experimenting with getting in the game in various ways. I imagine that you have too.

In reflecting on my own particular experiences and the public discourse surrounding these topics of impact, call, etc., I have come to believe that we could do a better job with this conversation. We often begin with dubious and unexamined assumptions and then proceed by asking questions that are not nearly as enlightening or helpful as other questions we might choose to ask instead.

This book is an effort to challenge some of those assumptions and offer some different questions, in the hope that some of the threads of these stories and ideas will weave into your own story and ideas and free you to have more of a positive impact.

I should mention here a couple of things that this book is *not* intended to be: it is not a strategy book. It is not intended to teach people how to mount effective social justice campaigns. I have a tentative plan to take on that book next (*Worldchanging 102?*), but it is not this one. This is a book about internalized social narratives—about challenging and changing the stories we tell ourselves and each other, some of which keep us paralyzed in the face of problems we could actually address if it weren't for our deep commitment to the idea of our own inadequacy. Before we have the conversation about *how* we are to go about influencing the world around us, we need to address the bigger question of whether that is even possible. It seems clear that many people do not believe that it is.

This is also not a book about politics, at least not in the sense that we generally use the word today. As we are endlessly reminded, we live in a particularly politically divisive time (though I'm not entirely convinced that there has ever been a time that was not politically divisive).

'Politics' is a blurry word, though. Here in the United States, it has come to mean the contest between the two major political parties. It often appears (and is occasionally blatantly admitted) that their primary goals are not to serve the nation but to defeat the other party. Though I am a strong advocate of political engagement, I am not terribly interested in party loyalty.

Politics is like dentistry. You're not really supposed to enjoy it, but the consequences of ignoring it are far worse than the pain of being involved.

In a broader sense, though, the political process, however flawed it may be, is the process by which we make decisions together about *what* matters and *who* matters. That definition includes not only the formal workings of government, but also public discourse, formal and informal media, individual participation through various direct and indirect means, and various forms of influence and power being wielded—appropriately or inappropriately—by the business world, non-profit organizations, civic groups, and others. That kind of politics interests me very much, and it is my duty and yours to be involved in that, no matter what country we live in.

To say that it interests me, by the way, is not the same thing as saying I like it. Politics is like dentistry. You're not really supposed to enjoy it, but the consequences of ignoring it are far worse than the pain of being involved. Where that analogy breaks down, of course, is that, unlike dentistry, if you ignore politics, it is not just you who suffers.

As Alexia Salvatierra and Peter Heitzel point out in their book *Faith Rooted Organizing*, "Democracy doesn't function effectively unless the people participate as active citizens—which is why we call our legislators 'representatives.' As surely as children's behavior reflects on their families, our legislators' behavior reflects on our communities."

That said, this book does not seem to me to be the right forum for arguing my political opinions. I know people of wisdom and integrity who disagree with me profoundly on various points, and I would love for them to be able to enjoy and employ the ideas presented in this book as much as people who tend to agree with me. I am conscious of the fact that I have been profoundly wrong about some things in my life, and I would therefore be ignoring the precedent of history to assume that I'm not wrong about anything now. I am a true believer in democracy. I think we make better decisions in community than we do individually and that the system works in proportion to how many of us are involved in making the decisions. It's inherently messy, but the extremes can only rule via the apathy of the reasonable, so on the whole, I think the more

With my son Mason in my water tower office in Srikakulam

people that join in the conversation, the better.

My political leanings, like my theology, will show through in places, I'm sure. That doesn't bother me too much, but I hope that no one will be snagged by perceived differences. It is not my intention to proselytize about either my faith or my politics.[1]

I suppose that the primary reason I've written this book is simply that several people over the years have asked me to. For about fifteen years now, I've been leading workshops and presenting keynotes that deal with the topics covered here, and it is from those talks and workshops that this book arose.

A few years ago, I taught one such workshop in Kentucky with a talented musician and activist named Mitch Barrett, and we co-billed in a concert that same evening. He is the first person I clearly remember asking me to write this stuff down, and I've finally decided to give it a shot. I hope you will find something of value in these words.

---

[1] People may be led to work for the common good from many worldviews and perspectives, both religious and secular, and I've been privileged to stand shoulder-to-shoulder in this work with people who hold many of them. For those who are interested, a study guide for Christian churches, co-written with my father, should be available soon after the book is published. I sincerely hope we will be able to offer study guides for other faiths and contexts as well. Go to worldchanging101.com for more information on those guides.

CHAPTER ONE

Changing My World

Tell me, what is it you plan to do with
your one wild and precious life?

— Mary Oliver

I knew I was a real 'road dog' not when I first woke up in a hotel and didn't know what town I was in, but when I woke up, didn't know what town I was in, and went to take a shower rather than taking the time to piece it together. I have spent most of the last 25 years on the road as a touring musician and songwriter, performing in 48 of the states in the U.S. and on five of the seven continents. Not knowing where I was had stopped surprising me; I knew it would come to me later.

Mornings have never been my specialty. Or rather, I prefer for them to come at the end of my day after a long night of music. Sunrises are lovely; then I happily go to bed. The experience of growing comfortable with not knowing where I was when I awoke, though, spoke more to the amount of time I was spending on the road than it did of my usual morning brain fog.

I wasn't in a hotel when I woke up on the morning of January 9, 2001. I was staying with my long-time friend Ann and her family. Though I did feel a bit disoriented, I knew these things: 1) I was in my friend's guest room in Leander, Texas, just north of Austin, well into a concert tour that was taking me across the South and over into New Mexico, 2) it was late morning and the sun was cutting in through the blinds, and 3) I didn't feel very good.

I had been out to dinner the night before with my friend Kristin, and by the time I woke up, Ann and her daughter Ellen, then a senior in high school, were off to work and school. I wrote in my journal a bit, took a shower, threw some clothes on, and got out my laptop to do a bit of bookkeeping. One not-so-glamorous side of being a professional independent musician is that in the eyes of the IRS, I run a small business, with all of the attendant bookkeeping that implies. Effectively, I'm an independent contractor, and they want to know all the details of what I make and spend. That means I do a fair amount of office work on the road. It's pretty rock star.

This particular day was not to be routine, though. As I got down to work plugging CD sales numbers into a spreadsheet, something strange began to happen. When I looked at the computer, I realized I was having a hard time seeing what was on the screen. It was as though I had been staring at a lightbulb and had a ghost image obscuring a spot near the middle of my vision. Looking at a particular cell in the spreadsheet seemed to be too difficult.

I moved from the couch where I had been sitting so that there wasn't a bright window behind me, thinking the glare might be the problem, but I was still having trouble. I was also feeling a bit nauseous, and I started to wonder if I might have picked up a bug. I felt a bit worse with each passing minute, so I gave up on the computer work.

Thinking it might calm my body and brain a bit, I took a bath, but I only felt more nauseous. And then things got even stranger. My arms began to go numb. It was as though they were 'asleep', but without the tingling of reawakening. I could use them, clumsily, but I couldn't feel much of anything. That lasted about twenty minutes, then gradually subsided. I started to get nervous; the flu had never done *that* to me before.

Ann was at work and I didn't have her number there, so I called Kristin to ask for it. I told her what was going on and she gave me the number. Because I was feeling pretty disoriented, I wanted to make sure that I had written the number down right. I read it back to her, but I read it out wrong, and she corrected me.

I tried again. To this day, I still believe I had written the digits down correctly, but somehow when I went to read them back to her, I was saying them wrong. It was as though I couldn't remember what the individual numbers were called. The numbers' names were jumbled. Kristin got scared, and so did I. She called Ann, and Ann called me.

While Ann was racing home from the city, my arms went numb again. As before, it lasted about twenty minutes. Before Ann got home, her daughter Ellen arrived home from high school. Ellen, who is now a physician, told me later that I was trying to talk to her but making no sense—I pointed to a chair and said 'wedding'.

Ann is a strong woman, doing her part to uphold the proud lineage of butt-kicking Texas matriarchs from which she is descended. She's a good person to have around in a crisis. We had become friends through the Kerrville Folk Festival, a magical mecca for songwriters and acoustic music enthusiasts that runs for 18 days each year on a big dusty ranch in the gentle hill country west of San Antonio. We camped there together each year for over a decade and kept in touch through the rest of the year. Over the years, she had become like a sister to me, and as her two daughters grew up, they have become good friends as well. I had the honor of officiating at Ellen's wedding a few years ago.

I couldn't come up with any hypothesis that wasn't catastrophic, and things were rapidly getting worse.

On the day in question, though, I wondered if these relationships and every other personal connection in my life might be drawing to a close. Ann got me in the car and blazed down the highway, talking on the phone with the emergency room at the nearest hospital.

On the way there, I tried to figure out what was happening to me. I was gradually losing my ability to use language, I was throwing up, and my arms kept going numb. Stroke? Brain tumor? Aneurism? Multiple Sclerosis? I couldn't come up with any hypothesis that wasn't catastrophic, and things were rapidly getting worse.

When I asked Ann to tell me her name she got really scared. I had been trying to think of it and couldn't, which was ridiculous. She was not just a casual friend. I didn't want to scare her, but it was both frustrating and terrifying that I couldn't get to it, so I asked her, and I managed to make the question understood. She said,

"David, it's Ann, I'm your good friend and I'm taking you to the hospital." I already understood everything but her name, though, and at that point I realized that I wasn't actually having too much trouble thinking, per se, it was just that the labels were all mixed up. I knew who and where I was and who I was with, but words weren't working for me. It wasn't as though I were drunk or losing consciousness, the primary neurological symptom was simply that I was losing access to language. I would later learn that this is called *aphasia*.

It seemed unlikely to me that this accelerating dysfunction was going to slow down or reverse. Therefore, it was likely that this was effectively the end of my life as I had known it. I might be accelerating toward a vegetative state, losing mental capacity and use of my limbs, or I might be simply dying, but in that moment it seemed impossible that things would ever return to what I had known as normal.

Ann squealed into the driveway of the emergency room, where we were met by a nurse with a wheelchair who immediately started asking me questions as he moved me bodily into the chair. I could still speak, though incoherently, but I couldn't answer, "What's seven plus three?" or tell him where my parents live. Meanwhile, Ann was talking a blue Texan streak, laying down the law with the nurse, insisting that drugs were not a part of this and they shouldn't waste time eliminating that possibility.

The next few hours are pretty hazy for me. I was quite dehydrated, and they put two bags of saline solution in my arm. They performed CAT scans, blood work, and a spinal tap, checking for each of the possible conditions I had thought of and a couple more that would be equally dire. Gradually I lost the ability to speak altogether, stopped throwing up, and lost consciousness.

After a few hours I woke up again, and while I was still disoriented and having language issues, things seemed to be less severe. As it turned out, the shape of this day was not a simple slope into complete dysfunction, but a bell curve, and the symptoms I had experienced gradually subsided over the next few hours.

Aside from a sore back and headache from the spinal tap,

I was mostly fine by the next morning. The doctor said that what I had experienced was a 'complex migraine'. Migraines, I learned, are not necessarily headaches at all. Headaches are just a common symptom. A migraine is a neurological condition which, according to the doctor who treated me that day, arises from spasms in the brain's blood vessels which prevent blood from getting to some parts of the brain. Other doctors argue that it is more of an electrical storm. A complex migraine, my doctor explained, is a migraine that results in neurological dysfunction.

What happened to me that day was certainly among the more dramatic events of my life. It was terrifying and bizarre, and then it was over. Twenty-four hours later I was a bit sore but basically fine. The next day I drove out of town in Dan the Tan Van, heading for New Mexico, where I had another couple of concerts booked.

Dan the Tan Van, my road companion in those days.

One of the many things I love about life on the road is the balance between that intensely interactive, vulnerable time with people at concerts and the complete solitude of driving for hours the next day. Obviously driving these days raises important questions of one's carbon footprint, but if it weren't for that, I would drive long distances just for the sake of the experience. Sometimes I long for the bygone tradition of Sunday afternoon family drives, hitting the road purely for the intrinsic value of the trip. As an introvert in an extroverted line of work, I need that road time to process, muse, and ponder, so that I'm ready to be fully present with the people I encounter in the next town, and so that I can try to figure out what the connections I've made so far mean for me, my art, and my spirit.

Driving down the long, straight highways of West Texas and New Mexico after that terrifying day in Austin, I had time to consider what had happened and its significance. I spent nearly two weeks musing and pondering about my medical misadventure before I wrote about it (I was a 'proto-blogger', beginning to write periodic Notes From the Road on my website—ironically, about three weeks before a man named John Barger coined the word 'weblog' in December of 1997).

This experience had changed me in several ways. First, I had spent a few hours thinking that my life was coming to a close, and I'd had time to consider what that meant to me. What struck me as I reflected on that experience was that, though I was certainly scared, I felt no sense of injustice, even in the dramatic moments when I thought I might be dying: I wasn't disappointed with the life I had lived up until then. While I wasn't eager to die at the age of 32, I couldn't complain that I hadn't had a rich ride. I was basically content. Even now, more than ten years later, that's a good thing to hold onto. I can only celebrate the intervening decade as 'bonus time'. It's like I got an extra life in a video game, except it's a real life.

The second and more unusual insight that grew out of that day's experience was much deeper for me. When I was gradually losing control and contact, I had a perception of my mind receding from me. It was such a vivid perception that it almost appeared to be happening in physical space. As I was losing consciousness in the hospital, there was something that seemed to be moving away from me in the darkness, like a ball of flickering blue light, which I understood to be my own intellect—my capacity for thought and reason.

What is interesting about that is that *my* perspective was not from within that mind looking back; my *mind* was moving away from *me*. What was left was not logic and thought, but existence. It was my deepest identity. My best interpretation is that this was my spirit, the deepest place that defines me. And for the first time in my life, I could almost tangibly perceive that as separate and distinct from my thinking mind. There was and is a deep comfort for me in having that almost visceral experience of my own spiritual identity—not what I think, but who I am, on a much deeper level than words, logic, or calculation, all of which had been stripped away.

The third observation, though, is the one that brings me to write this book. I couldn't help but notice, after simply celebrating the joy of still having a future, that the two things that had been taken from me that day were my *hands* and my *words*.

At the time, I was celebrating my first decade of making a living by playing guitar and singing self-penned songs. It was powerful for me to consider that on that day, it was these two things in particular that I had lost: my ability to hold a guitar and feel the tips of my fingers pressing into steel strings, and my capacity to choose and use words, whether for their meaning or their musicality. The extremely personal tools of my art and my trade had been taken away.

And then they were returned.

The question may as well have been written in neon in the sky: "What will you do with these hands and these words?" Or, as the poet Mary Oliver has written, "Tell me, what is it you plan to do with your one wild and precious life?" I had been wrestling with that question in a more general and ambiguous sense for many years, but now it was suddenly brought into searing clarity, forcing me to deeply interrogate my own days and the motivations that drive how I fill them. It was another gift to me, if a painful one, and I continue to receive it and to feel its sting.

I suspect that very few of us find, when we look closely at our lives, that our beliefs and our actions match up neatly. I certainly saw a gulf between the two in my own life, and this experience forced me to face it. In the years since that misadventure in Texas, I've reoriented my life somewhat, though certainly imperfectly, wrestling with my own sense of call and exploring where my own particular joy and gifts can be useful in the world.

For a decade, my entire adult life at that point, I had been traveling around singing hopeful songs about better ways to live our lives, be present, and love each other—and I think that matters. Music can open our hearts in ways that words by themselves seldom can. But I felt a restlessness that wouldn't abate, a compulsion to work on making a difference that I could see. I wanted to explore more direct forms of change.

Gradually, I began to more actively seek out ways to have a more tangible positive impact on the world around me. In 2004, my wife Deanna and I co-founded a non-profit that supports school and library projects in Guatemala. In 2008, I suspended my music career and moved to Australia to pursue a masters in International Studies, Peace, and Conflict Resolution as a Rotary World Peace Fellow. The following year I spent three months in rural southern India, working with a Gandhian sustainable development organization. In 2011, I began a six-year stint on the American Friends Service Committee (AFSC)'s Nobel Peace Prize Nominating Task Group. In recent years, I have been doing a lot more speaking and writing in an effort to methodically encourage people to actively address the problems they see rather than fall into the common pattern of just complaining about them. More recently, I've been to jail a couple of times for non-violent civil disobedience, protesting misguided policies that are hurting people in my state, North Carolina. In the midst of all this, I've engaged in many smaller efforts, as most of us do from time to time.

My medical mishap was a gift to me because it made me seriously evaluate my life. A sudden awareness of the finitude of one's life naturally leads to questions about how one should spend it. I can't claim, by a long shot, that my beliefs and my daily life now match up perfectly, but I hope I'm narrowing the gap a little, and the struggle to do so is itself enriching.

Of course, the question of what one should do leads directly to the question of what one *can* do—what we are capable of. Like most people, I suspect, I open up the paper or click through the news online with a sense of malaise that sometimes borders on despair. The problems we face—as individuals, as families, as communities, as nations, and as a planet—are significant, large, and insidious. It is sometimes hard to imagine how anyone could have much of an impact, much less how *I* could.

Beyond this sense of overwhelmed paralysis, even if we can imagine engaging, questions remain regarding how and where to begin. Where should I start? What's most important? What, specifically, should *I* do? We will wrestle with those *This book doesn't seek to recruit you to any causes but your own, though I do unabashedly hope to recruit you to those.* questions and others in the following pages, but I don't pretend that they are easy questions to answer.

I do believe, however, that you can have a significant impact. That's not a starry-eyed, hopeful-but-naive statement; it is a conclusion I have been led to through years of wrestling with the questions that inspired this book. I know it to be true for many reasons, some of which are laid out in the chapters that follow. Our cultural assumptions about our individual roles in steering large-scale change, how change comes about, and who causes that change are often misguided. I want to spend a bit of time turning these assumptions over and holding them up to the light to see whether they are true or not—and, with that knowledge, how they should influence our daily choices.

Though this book endeavors to be an honest, reality-based look at how things change and what we can hope to accomplish, it is also unapologetically hopeful. Part of my goal is to argue that those two characteristics, honest and hopeful, are not necessarily mutually exclusive.

Historian Howard Zinn argues in the first chapter of his *People's History of the United States* that all historians necessarily bring their own "selection, simplification, [and] emphasis" to their subject matter. He implies that the most honest approach to presenting history is to clearly state one's own biases and goals. Starting from the same set of facts, each of us naturally tends to see different pieces as important and emphasize those.

With that in mind, I will explicitly name my own agenda: I want my five-year-old son and the rest of his generation to grow up in a world that is growing and healing rather than one that is tearing itself apart, socially, politically, and physically.

In order to accomplish that, I need to convince you to lend your energy to creating that world. And in order to move toward that, I am writing this book. In it, I hope to 1) challenge some wrong-headed ideas about how change happens, 2) convince you of your own capacity to have an impact, and 3) offer some questions to help you discern your own calling—how and where you can offer your gifts and energy to a movement of people trying to shift things in healthier and more sustainable directions.

I am not, however, trying to win you over to my causes or positions. This book doesn't seek to recruit you to any causes but your own, though I do unabashedly hope to recruit you to those. I don't know what you are passionate about, but I believe that if more of us actually take action on the issues that concern us, we will all be better off. Our most dangerous threat, in the end, is apathy.

CHAPTER TWO

What Are You Talking About?

*We believe that we know something about the things
themselves when we speak of trees, colors, snow, and flowers;
and yet we possess nothing but metaphors for things—
metaphors which correspond in no way to the original entities.*

— Friedrich Nietzsche

Communication is a miracle. Even to speak to a friend in the same room, patterns of sound—variations in amplitude and frequency, thick and thin waves of air, produced by complex biological processes involving tiny patterned electrical pulses and chemical signals triggering subtle muscle contractions and expansions—travel from mouth to ear, where they are decoded and structured into words. These words, in turn, are fairly arbitrary code systems for meanings (of which most words have many), which are strung together to represent ideas. It is not surprising that we sometimes misunderstand each other; really, it is shocking that we ever communicate at all.

The German philosopher Johann Georg Hamann took it even farther, saying, "Language is not only the foundation for the whole faculty of thinking, but the central point also from which proceed the misunderstandings of reason by herself." Even in our own minds, even without external communication, words not only give us the tools to think, they are also the main thing that trips us up.

Because of that, I think it may be worthwhile to define a few of the central terms in this book, not because they are complex and academic (this is not that kind of book), but because they are so common that we seldom take the time to consider exactly what we mean when we use them. Each of the words I want to consider has multiple meanings in English, and my point in taking a quick look at them is not to argue that one definition is the correct one, but simply to outline what *I* mean when I use them, in the hope of diminishing the chances that we will misunderstand each other.

Hope & Optimism

Václav Havel was the last president of Czechoslovakia and the first president of the Czech Republic. He was a successful poet and playwright as well as a dissident activist— the leader of the country's non-violent transition from Communism to democracy that came to be known as the 'Velvet Revolution'. It is rare for a true artist and poet to also be a head of state, and Havel offered a great deal of wisdom from that extremely unusual vantage point.

Hope, it seems to me, is both an active choice and a choice to be active.

One of my favorite quotations from Havel, or anyone else for that matter, is this: *"Hope is not prognostication, it is an orientation of the spirit."*

Hope, in Havel's estimation, has nothing to do with prediction. "Hope is definitely not the same thing as optimism," Havel writes elsewhere. It is not the conviction that something will turn out well, but the certainty that something makes sense, regardless of how it turns out."

Rather, hope is the conscious decision to live toward the world you would like to see, to take action to move closer to a better way, regardless of your chances of achieving your goal. The historian Howard Zinn writes:

> *To be hopeful in bad times is not being foolishly romantic. It is based on the fact that human history is a history not only of competition and cruelty but also of compassion, sacrifice, courage, kindness... The future is an infinite succession of presents, and to live now as we think human beings should*

live, in defiance of all that is bad around us, is itself a marvelous victory.

Living in hope is not a matter of believing that things will be OK, or that the good guys eventually win. Hope begins with an honest assessment of a given situation, but it grows into a conscious choice to lend your own energy to move that situation in a better direction. It is an 'orientation of the spirit', and the movements of our spirits inevitably inform our actions. 'Orientation' implies direction, which way you intend to move.

Hope, it seems to me, is both an active choice and a choice to be active.

Activist & Protestor

What do you picture when you hear the word 'activist'? In my *Worldchanging 101* workshops, I like to ask people what images—specifically images, not ideas—come to mind when they hear that word. The responses vary a bit, but there are some things that come up nearly every time: marching, holding signs, shouting. Then I ask what affect, what emotional tone, comes to mind, and pretty consistently, the first thing I hear is 'angry'.

So there it is: an activist is an angry protestor, marching in the street holding a sign.

There is no question that this is one kind of activist, and there is a time and place to march in the streets holding signs. I have certainly done that, and likely will again.

I want to be abundantly clear, though, that when I say *activist*, this is not what I mean.

An *-ism*, according to Merriam-Webster, is "the act, practice, or process of doing something." Their first definition for *active* is "doing things that require physical movement and energy."

So activism is, more or less, the act of doing something that requires physical movement and energy. In other words, taking some action. Any action. 'Active-ism' is the opposite of 'passive-ism', doing *nothing* in the face of a problem.

In this book, when I say activism, that's what I mean: taking any action whatsoever to address a problem that exists outside of yourself (if the problem is on the inside of your skin, it's personal growth). Whether that's talking to the manager at the grocery store about a problem you see, making a donation to an organization you believe in, writing a letter to the editor, visiting the elderly man down the street because he seems to be cut off from his community, or clicking an online petition.[2] If you are taking any action at all to address a problem external to yourself, you are an activist.[3]

The stereotypical image of an angry activist marching in the street or chained to a gate or tree is so pervasive that it can be hard to replace in our own minds. But that definition is misguided.

Marches and civil disobedience, while sometimes extremely effective, are not always the best strategies available. Those types of actions may not be your calling, but that doesn't mean you are not an activist. I suspect that if you've read this far, you are the kind of person who has at least taken some action in your life to address a problem. Please try to remember as you read this book that when I use the word 'activist', I am referring to you.

Anger & Hatred

In everyday conversation, I have found that many people fail to distinguish between anger and hatred, or that we consider

---

[2] The term 'slacktivist', referring to someone who may hold forth with strong opinions on Facebook or click online petitions but doesn't actually show up to do much beyond that, has recently become popular among some activists. It's a clever and amusing term, but it is also self-congratulatory and counter-productive. If people have a toe in the water of being active but haven't waded in yet, they don't need to be shamed, they need to be thanked for their effort, encouraged, and shown the next step.

[3] *Passive-ism* should not be confused with *pacifism*, though it often is. Pacifism comes from root words that mean 'peace' and 'making'. *Pax* means 'peace', and *facere* is the fundamental action verb of Latin, like *hacer* in Spanish or *faire* in French, meaning 'to do' or 'to make'. Therefore, pacifism is fundamentally active: it is utterly impossible to be a passive pacifist. *Passive*, in contrast, comes from the Latin word *pati*, meaning to suffer or endure, which is what people tend to do when they are passive in the face of a serious problem.

them points on a continuum, with hatred being an extreme form of anger. That is not what I mean when I use these words.

Anger is an emotion. It often arises when injustice is perceived, and that is a natural and understandable response—maybe even laudable. Our anger may be directed at an unjust situation, at a person or institution that is maintaining or encouraging an injustice, or even at ourselves for our passivity in the face of injustice. Anger, in and of itself, is natural, and it is not a bad thing. For the most part, we don't get to choose how we feel, and we are not responsible for those feelings. We are entirely responsible, however, for what we do with them. Anger can be a powerful motivator for constructive action, at least for a little while. Over time, it tends to calcify into hatred.

In other words, anger is an important place to visit from time to time, but a pretty rotten place to live.

In other words, anger is an important place to visit from time to time, but a pretty rotten place to live.

Hatred, as opposed to anger, involves wishing harm. It is entirely possible to be very angry with someone you love, but to truly hate someone is in direct contrast with truly loving them. By the definitions I'm using here, love and hatred cannot coexist. Passionate infatuation and hatred, yes. But love and hatred are mutually exclusive. Love and anger, on the other hand, are actually quite a powerful combination when it comes to worldchanging.

Love & Affection

That brings us to one of the most ambiguous and broadly defined words I know: *love*. I use this word to describe how I feel about my parents, how I feel about my wife, and how I feel about Indian food. Civil Rights heroes in the United States also used the word love to describe their disciplined response to police and others who would beat and abuse them as they engaged in nonviolent civil disobedience. These are drastically different definitions.

In casual conversation, we tend to use the word love to describe a point on a continuum of affection. At one end there is loathing, a bit over from that is dislike, indifference is in the middle, then like, and at the far end, love.

I need to be abundantly clear, however, that this is not the kind of love I'm talking about when I use the word in this book (which I will do sparingly, but occasionally). In fact, love, in the present context, is not an emotion at all.

As with 'hope', when I use the word love in this book, I will be referring to an active choice rather than a feeling. Love is the decision to hold up another's well-being and dignity, regardless of how you feel about that person. It is about how we treat people, sometimes not *because* of our feelings but rather *in spite* of them.

> In fact, love, in the present context, is not an emotion at all.

In offering that defi-nition, I shouldn't discount the fact that it is entirely possible to nourish and cultivate certain emotions. Both Gandhi and leaders of non-violent resistance efforts in the U.S. Civil Rights Movement trained vigorously so that they could learn to redirect their feelings and to perceive the humanity even in people who were actively doing them harm, and, yes, to *feel* love for them.

John Lewis was a student leader in the U.S. Civil Rights Movement and one of the primary organizers of the Nashville lunch counter sit-ins in 1960. He and his compatriots trained vigorously for a full year before they acted out their famous nonviolent transforming initiatives, sitting at "Whites only" lunch counters and refusing to leave when asked to.[4] Years later, John Lewis would

---

4 The current writing convention is that all racial classifications are capitalized except for 'white', and sometimes, 'black'. That seems disturbingly inconsistent to me. I am capitalizing all racial classifications in this book because it seems more clear and more equitable. Whiteness is also a social location, and I don't want to support a convention which seems to say that white is normal and everything else is 'other'. Race, though it is a social construct and not a genetic reality, plays a big role in the functioning of our world, and how we have the conversation about it is almost as important as what we say.

use this same training to continue to march forward in nonviolence even as state police were beating him and others with batons on the Edmund Pettus bridge in Selma.

Lewis argues that the ability to feel love for his attackers is fundamental to his nonviolence. In his 2012 book *Across That Bridge*, Lewis described training for civil disobedience:

> *...for those of us who accepted [nonviolence] not simply as a tactic but as a way of authentically living our lives—our sole purpose was, in fact, love. We would settle for the proceeds of justice and equal rights, but the force guiding our involvement was the desire to redeem the souls of our brothers and sisters who were beguiled by the illusion of superiority, taken in and so distorted by their false god that they were willing to destroy any contradiction of that faith. If we were pawns of an unjust system, they were also so complicit in their own degradation that they justified wrong as a service to the right.*

Lewis and others got to that place by cultivating their compassion, which etymologically means "suffering with," in order to perceive the humanity of their oppressors. Through rigorous training and study, he and his colleagues in the struggle learned to actually *feel* differently about people who were doing them harm. That's pretty extraordinary, especially when you remember that these words were spoken by a man who was beaten bloody and unconscious on many occasions.

But that's a pretty high bar to set, and quite a dramatic context in which to examine nonviolence. This kind of moral ascendance and physical sacrifice is not what I'm asking of you or myself in this book, at least not as a starting place. So many of these heroic stories, as we read them in the history books, leave out the years of small, incremental steps that led ordinary people to such heroic actions. I don't want to make the same mistake here.

As a starting place, I think it is enough to ask of ourselves that we love people through our actions—including speech, gesture, and expression—whether or not we can summon the feelings to go with that. Love as an active choice is hard enough, and a sufficient goal in itself. The danger in asking too much of ourselves is that when we are not able to achieve immediately what our heroes achieved over many years, we will feel like we have failed.

It may well be that the emotional perspective will follow the lived experience. I think that is what happened with Lewis and his companions. For now, though, let's bite off a chewable piece.

What is abundantly clear, at any rate, is that loving someone is not simply an extreme version of liking them. In fact, it is sometimes our job to love people we don't like at all.

Aid & Justice

I often have the opportunity to lead conversations with faith communities about social justice work, and when I do, I often ask them what kind of justice work they are engaged in.

Generally, the answers that come back do not describe justice work, but aid work. Both are important, and they sometimes overlap, but there is a difference, and it is important to make the distinction.

The best story I've heard to illustrate that difference has been told by many different people with slight variations, and I'm not sure to whom it should be attributed. Here's what happens in the story:

> One day a woman was taking a walk. Enjoying the solitude and peace of strolling beside a river, she heard a splashing sound and turned her head to see if a duck was landing or a fish jumping.
>
> Instead, she saw a baby floating down the river. It was thrashing and trying to breathe and clearly in great danger. Immediately, she plunged into the cold river and got the baby. She brought it to the bank and tried to warm and comfort it while it choked out water and cried, all the while looking around for some explanation or someone else to help.
>
> Then she heard another splash and turned around to

see another baby floating down the river. She was doubly shocked, but the situation demanded quick action, so she set the first baby down on the riverbank and dove back into the water to get the second baby.

She hadn't even made it back to the shore when a third baby came floating downstream. This time, though, someone else was coming along the path, so she shouted out for him to come help while she plunged back into the cold river for the third rescue.

The woman quickly informed the man who had just walked up as to what was happening, and before she was explaining what little she knew, sure enough, here came a fourth baby. The man had a phone and started calling friends to come down and bring blankets, formula, and whatever else they could think of. In the meantime, the two of them continued to pull babies from the river.

Over time, lots of people came to help. They brought bassinets and tents and diapers, but the babies kept coming, so eventually they started raising money and built a permanent structure beside the river to deal with the steady flow of babies. They had developed a solid volunteer crew and a long-term plan for feeding and housing the babies. They obtained their 501c3 tax exempt status from the government. They had almost started to feel like they were catching up when one day an older woman walked into the building, looked around with a stern expression, threw her head back, and shouted for everyone to stop and be quiet.

Shocked, they all did so, and when she had everyone's full attention, she looked around the room and firmly but quietly said, "Don't you think it's time we went upstream to see who is throwing them in?"

That story, while fictitious, provides a helpful illustration of the difference between aid work and justice work. Aid work is about meeting people's needs. Justice work is about challenging the systems that make them needy.

I should also say that I have sometimes heard this story told with an undercurrent of superiority by people who do justice work—implying that justice work is the wiser, nobler, and more effective path. But if everyone at the baby shelter had stopped what they were doing and marched upstream, the babies coming down the river that day would have drowned.

Aid work and justice work are both necessary. The former tends to be more short-term and the latter more long-term, but they both have the potential to serve people who need help and support.

Aid work is about meeting people's needs. Justice work is about challenging the systems that make them needy.

Aid and justice work can also overlap and be mutually supportive. I've found that this is sometimes the case with communities working with people who have no shelter. Some of these communities take on both the work of helping people find what they need for material sustenance and safety and of educating and challenging local governments and the larger society on the problems they are dealing with and the structural causes of those problems.

My friends at the Open Door Community in Atlanta, for example, were growing weary of bailing their friends out of jail for urinating in alleys. As my friend Ed Loring at the Open Door tells it, the city had no public toilets until 2000. That meant that people who had no homes to go to and no money to spend in businesses that might allow them access to facilities also had nowhere to relieve themselves. When they did what was necessary, they were arrested, in spite of having no other practical options.

The Open Door community not only made their home available for showers and toilets, they also began to advocate for more public toilets. On several occasions in the nineties they marched down to the City Hall and had demonstrations, giving speeches, singing, and reading scripture in Mayor Andrew Young's office while seated on a porcelain perch that they had brought with them. They worked to meet people's needs and at the same time challenged the systems that made them needy (and did so with a sense of humor). Eventually, more people took up the cause, and finally the city built public toilets.

These days it seems to be in fashion to lionize justice work and denigrate aid work. Stories of soup kitchens that categorize everyone involved into 'helper' or 'helped', or charities that serve from a distance without sharing stories and human fellowship, are not hard to find, and those approaches are certainly problematic.

Aid work has the potential to destroy dignity and entrench hierarchical and sometimes hegemonic systems and values. In my experience, however, justice work has that potential as well. Both aid and justice work can be carried out in ways that demean all involved and tokenize certain people while celebrating others. Both, too, can build relationship, nourish dignity, and address problems in meaningful, sustainable ways that build capacity and mutual respect on all sides. It is tempting, but unwise, to paint all of it with a broad brush.

These two different approaches, sometimes mutually supportive and sometimes in tension, are both necessary. Part of our work is to discern our own roles within each, and how to do them both well.

Peace & Placidity

I referred earlier to Civil Rights hero John Lewis, who headed up the Student Nonviolent Coordinating Committee (SNCC), the student wing of the non-violent movement led by Dr. Martin Luther King, Jr. Since 1987, he has served as a United States Congressman representing Georgia's fifth congressional district.

In early 2009, just before heading to Australia to begin my masters degree, I had the opportunity to meet him and spend some time in conversation. Representative Lewis was coming to Western North Carolina, where I live, to speak at the Montreat Conference Center. My friend Wade Burns is a long-time friend of Lewis', having worked on integration issues in Atlanta with him, sometimes in intense and dangerous situations.

Wade was heading to the airport to pick Representative Lewis up and asked me if I wanted to ride along. We met Lewis at the airport and, after a brief reunion of old friends and an introduction, headed for the parking lot. Representative Lewis wouldn't let either of us help with his bag, nor would he sit in the front when we got to the van. Wade smiled at this and said that he wanted the two of us to have some time for conversation, so John Lewis and I sat together in the back seat and talked, with Wade quietly playing the chauffeur and listening.

> The work of peacemaking is not about ending conflict, it is about approaching conflict in ways that are constructive rather than destructive.

It was an extraordinary gift to me, and a generous thing for Wade to consciously give up that time with his long-time friend so that we could talk. Later that evening, we had dinner together with a few other guests at Wade's home, but for that time in the van, I had John Lewis' full attention. I didn't waste it.

Representative Lewis wanted to know about me and what I was working on, so I briefly told him about my music and my workshops, my brand-new baby boy and the fact that I would be packing up my family in a couple of weeks to move to Australia to pursue a masters degree in peace work as a Rotary World Peace Fellow. The conversation naturally turned to peace work and then to some common misunderstandings about that pursuit. Chief among those is the idea that peace is the lack of conflict.

It was, and sometimes still is, a common criticism of John Lewis, Martin Luther King, Jr., Rosa Parks and their compatriots in the Civil Rights Movement that they were hardly peacemakers; after all, everywhere they went conflict and violence seemed to erupt! However, that critique betrays a shallow understanding of peace.

The kind of peace work that these people were involved

John Lewis and me, back when I had hair.

with had to do with structural violence—violence that is built into systems and damages people in ways that are equally destructive, but far more subtle than direct violence. The status quo in the presence of injustice or unresolved injury, even where overt violence might be tamped down, can hardly be called peaceful.

Lewis said to me, "Peace is not the absence of conflict; conflict is often necessary on the way to justice." Those words, coming from a man who had willingly and courageously endured significant violence, had the full weight of history behind them.

The other thing Representative Lewis said to me that I will never forget made all the hairs on my arms stand up.[5] He said, "Dr. King used to say to me, 'Sometimes you have to turn the world upside down in order to set it right.'"

So peace is not placidity. Sometimes the work of peacemaking

---

[5] I try to pay attention when that happens, since it's one of the things you can't fake. I consider it a signal from my subconscious that something important is happening.

involves *revealing* a conflict that is woven into a situation. Bringing it out into the open so that we can deal with it. That can look like creating tension. In fact, people who work for justice are constantly accused of 'stirring up trouble'. But the trouble is there already. In order to heal it, we have to give it light and air.

Truthfully, the noun *peace* is not nearly as interesting to me as the gerund form: *peacemaking*. I'm not interested in a static, unachievable, utopian ideal as much as I am interested in discerning what my role is in moving myself and the world around me a bit more in a positive direction.

Conflict is an inevitable part of being human, and as Lewis points out, it is not necessarily a bad thing. The work of peacemaking is not about ending conflict, it is about approaching conflict in ways that are *con*structive rather than *de*structive.

The key word in that sentence is 'approaching'.

CHAPTER THREE

Good Luck With That

*While I am not optimistic, I am hopeful. By this I mean that
hope, as opposed to cynicism and despair, is the sole
precondition for a new and better life; and hope arouses,
as nothing else can arouse, a passion for the possible.*

— William Sloan Coffin

January 20, 2009, a couple of weeks after I met John Lewis, was inauguration day in the United States. My wife Deanna, my friend and office manager MJ, my parents, and I gathered to watch Barack Obama take the oath of office. No matter how one feels about the presidency that followed, that moment was undeniably historic, and for me, it was deeply inspiring.

We watched it in an empty house with almost no furniture remaining, crowding around my laptop, my mother holding our ten-week-old son. We celebrated the election of a candidate who we believed would turn the country in a better direction than the one in which we had been heading. Then we closed the laptop, put our suitcases in the car, drove to the airport, and moved to Australia.

President Obama and I were both embarking on new chapters that day, though mine, needless to say, was on a much smaller scale. Many good and bad decisions were yet to come for both of us, but in both cases the day was significant, even with nothing yet accomplished, just because of the choice to begin.

A great deal had already changed for me from the same date two years before. In early 2007, I was celebrating 16 years on the road as a full-time musician. I had developed a base of listeners on three continents who were coming out to shows, buying my CDs, sending lovely notes from time to time, telling their friends about my music, and supporting me, both financially and as an artist. After getting through the initial inevitable years of starving musicianship, I had something that many musicians more talented than I am never get to have—a music career.

I was also married to a smart, strong, kind, and beautiful woman who supported my art while still having her own life and enough confidence in our relationship to allow me to be gone a great deal of the time. In spite of the travel, we agree that we had more 'quality time' in those years than most couples do because when I came home we set aside everything else just to be together.

We were pretty close to having paid for our little house in the mountains of Western North Carolina. We had family nearby and friends to raise an occasional glass with. In short, things were working.

And that's when I decided to walk away.

I had heard from a friend about the Rotary Peace Fellowship, a generous academic fellowship for a master's degree in Peace and Conflict Resolution, and the idea had snapped my head around. My friend had just completed a master's degree funded by the Rotary Foundation at the University of Bradford in England, and it sounded like an extraordinary experience.

I was amazed that such a program existed, but I was even more amazed at my own reaction to hearing about it: against all precedent, it tempted me away from the professional path I had been happily walking for my entire adult life. I certainly had plenty of days when I was weary of the road, but on the whole, I was happy in my work. I was among the very few musicians whose dream had come true.

Still, it felt like this was the next chapter for me. Not in any practical sense, but in an almost mystical one. It was simply clear. It was as if I had come to a corner and could suddenly see around it—and there was the road. I had been heading in that direction all along but couldn't see it until I got to the corner.

To be fair, this direction wasn't entirely new. During my undergraduate years in the late eighties, I attended James Madison University in Harrisonburg, Virginia. I took one music theory class and barely passed it, but I was fascinated by my psychology classes and ended up majoring in that. It wasn't until I had been there a while, though, that I found my real passion.

I don't remember how I first came across alternative conflict resolution work, but once I did, I was hooked. I ended up doing an independent study and interning at the Community Mediation Center, where I was exposed to some amazing peacemakers doing substantive work in their own community to help heal wounds in families, between neighbors, in the business community, and elsewhere.

I was so impressed with these people and that experience. I watched the work they did each day, learned about mediation and conflict resolution, helped put on trainings, and even engaged in some of the mediation myself. I

Im short, things were working. And that's when I decided to walk away.

was quickly converted, and was amazed to discover that there are more effective ways to approach conflict than the ones we usually turn to, and yet we so seldom use them. Mediation is demonstrably better at resolving most kinds of conflicts than litigation is,[6] whether we measure the results in satisfaction of the parties to the conflict, durability of the agreements, or by a variety of other measures. In those days (the late eighties), mediation was just moving into the mainstream, and I became a passionate advocate for it.

It was in those same years, however, that I started performing publicly. I had been playing guitar in the solitude of my bedroom for many years, but in college I worked up the courage to play an open mic, and I was amazed and thrilled to find that people didn't boo me off the stage. As I started to perform more around town, I was even more surprised to realize that people were reacting positively to some of the songs I had written myself, not just the

---

[6] I'm not picking on lawyers here. An attorney once pointed out to me at the National Restorative Justice Conference that litigation *is* alternative conflict resolution, and he is quite right. It's a significant step in the right direction from violence and deserves credit as such. Mediation, I believe, takes another healthy step in the right direction.

standard canon of folk/pop that made up most of my repertoire in those days. I spent a semester abroad in Paris in the second half of my junior year and ended up traveling for a few weeks after it was over, playing on street corners in order to have money for food. And I didn't starve.

When I graduated from college, I felt strongly pulled in two different directions, and the two vocations were incompatible. On the one hand, there was mediation, which had become a passion for me, and felt like a way that I might have a positive influence in the world. On the other, there was music, an even more unlikely way to make a living, and one about which I was equally passionate. In the years I'd been playing informally, I had occasionally seen tears in the eyes of people listening when I played my own songs. It seemed like my music might actually matter too.

In the light of some significant encouragement (some of which is outlined in stories which appear later in this book), I decided to give myself two years to see if I could make a living playing music. I got a side job that didn't require much brain power and didn't run the risk of becoming a passion for me: moving chairs and setting up A/V gear in the Assembly Inn in Montreat, North Carolina—the very hotel where my parents had met working their own summer jobs nearly forty years before. I had worked there through the summer in a job that had tested my limits in various ways, but at the end of the summer I switched to manual labor. Four months later, as the tourist season wound down, there wasn't much work left for me to do there, and I began my life as a full-time musician.

The trajectory of an independent music career usually doesn't have a lot of spikes in it. It is mostly a matter of longevity, connecting with a base of people over many years who relate to what you're doing and building relationships. Those relationships have sustained me both emotionally and financially through the support of faithful fans and friends who continue to invite me into various opportunities to speak and perform and who keep coming to the shows, even though they have heard some of those songs many times before.

My music career is a bit of an anomaly, though. My mother told me that she heard a story on NPR a few years ago in which they interviewed someone who had done a study on how many people who set out to have a career in music actually get to have one. That researcher came up with 1 in 500.

I got to be that one. For years I made my living simply by playing self-penned songs for mostly small audiences, traveling in progressively wider circles until I had developed small but passionate followings in the United States as well as in Australia, New Zealand, Germany.

But I never lost my passion for peace work. While I was traveling in Europe, I would go to places where significant conflicts were taking place and meet people who were engaged with those issues on a daily basis.

I learned what I could learn by watching and listening, and I shone what light I could shine by playing songs and telling stories.

On one trip, I went to northern Ireland[7] and met with people doing front lines peace work there, some working with war widows and orphans, others with youth, trying to break down the persistent cultural and historical barriers between Protestants and Catholics.

On another trip, I performed for United Nations peacekeeping troops at Eagle Base in Tuzla, Bosnia, then spent a few days in Sarajevo, where I connected with peacemakers doing reconciliation work in that troubled time and place. I learned what I could learn by watching and listening, and I shone what light I could shine by playing songs and telling stories.

I kept looking for ways to connect more substantially with peace work, which had remained a passion for me. I couldn't

---

[7]This is not a typo (my editor would never let me do that!). I'm following the lead of my good friend, peacemaker, film critic, and author Gareth Higgins, from Belfast. He explains in his excellent book Cinematic States that he chooses not to capitalize the 'N' in northern Ireland, "because we still can't agree on what to call my divided home."

see how it was compatible, though. Mediation requires a steady presence and availability. Music, at least the way I was approaching it, requires a great deal of travel and a lifestyle almost devoid of routine.

So I mostly gave my energy to music, putting out ten CDs over 18 years and performing about 2,000 concerts around the world. Each year went better than the last in terms of opportunities and finances. It was a good life. With the help of a friend who gave me an amazing deal and a small inheritance from my grandparents,

As a culture, we have some commonly held beliefs about this idea of working to change the world for the better. Foremost among them is that it is naive.

I began buying a little house. When I met my wife Deanna, I was even able to help her out with her student loans.

There was no practical reason that I should walk away. After years of living very simply and cheaply, I finally had a bit of breathing room. Still, when I heard about the Rotary World Peace Fellowship, I had to pursue it.

If I got it, it would require moving to another country. Each year, the Rotary Foundation chooses 50 people from all over the world to pursue master's degrees in Peace Studies or a related field at one of five prominent universities around the world and 50 more to do a three-month certificate program in Thailand. The Rotary Foundation generously provides tuition, living expenses, funding for independent field study, and even transportation there and back.

At that point I didn't even know which of the four Rotary World Peace Centers I would attend if selected: in Argentina, Japan, England, or Australia[8] (the rules require that Fellows study in countries other than their own, so the two in the U.S. at that time

---

[8] The Rotary Peace Center in Argentina has now been replaced by a program in Uppsala, Sweden. For more information on the Rotary Peace Fellowship, visit rotary.org/en/peace-fellowships.

were off-limits). More than that, I had no reason to be confident that I would be awarded the fellowship at all, given that applicants had to rise through a rigorous selection process and were chosen from throughout the entire world.

Even so, I announced the beginning of a year-long farewell tour that would take me to many of the places I had come to love as a musician and give me a chance to say some important goodbyes. I felt so strongly drawn to this new path that I announced my 'retirement' as a musician, in spite of the very real possibility that I would not be awarded the fellowship. If I didn't get it, I reasoned, it was because some other avenue of peace work would open to me. What I knew was that I needed to focus on this work for a while, and in order to do that, I had to lay down my guitar. I love music too much to do just a little of it on the side, so I knew that if I was going to seriously pursue my other vocation in peace work, it would need my full attention.

I had some friends who supported my new direction. Though some were admittedly unsure, they patted me on the back and wished me well. There were others who were simply baffled, and some expressed misgivings. Others, rather than patting me on the back, patted me on the head, at least figuratively. 'Peace work' sounds like a rather silly place to put one's energy, and I had put a lot of work into my music career.

The most common response I got was from well-meaning friends and acquaintances who raised an eyebrow, smiled with an expression that was warm if somewhat sardonic, and said, "Peace? Good luck with that."

As a culture, we have some commonly held beliefs about this idea of working to change the world for the better. Foremost among them is that it is naive. According to the popular narrative, such idealistic effort is born of a childish perspective that people are basically good and reasonable, joined with a sheltered ignorance of the hard cruelty of the 'real world'. Experience and maturity, the logic goes, will cure the idealists of their foolish delusions.

And beyond the perceived naiveté of the would-be world changers, there is the fundamentally chaotic and destructive nature of the world itself. "Look at the world!" the skeptics quite reasonably cry. People have been trying to end war and poverty for centuries, and yet the world is riddled with war and crippled by poverty. The lesson they draw is this: *You can't change the world.*

This sounds so self-evident as to be banal. And how ridiculous does it sound to suggest the opposite? Here's an experiment: Next time you run into a friend at the grocery store and they ask what you're up to these days, look them in the eyes and say, without irony, "Oh, y'know, I'm changing the world."

There will likely be some combination of chuckling, nervous subject-changing, and possibly an urgent matter in the produce aisle that your friend suddenly needs to attend to. Such a statement sounds foolish, comical, or slightly unbalanced. Your friend is likely to walk away wondering if you inhaled too much exhaust on your way in from the parking lot.

The skeptics really seem to have a point, don't they? Isn't it naive, even mildly delusional, to think you can change the world?

And even if the world *does* change, even if it moves a bit in response to our efforts to change it, still: look at the world! In spite of generations of leaders claiming they stand for peace and thousands of movements around the world working for it, the planet is dripping with violence.[9]

Hope, peacemaking, and efforts to effect change are not rooted in denial of the gritty reality of the world, though. They are rooted in the observation that we in fact can have a positive impact and that it is irresponsible and self-defeating not to try.

The nihilist position that we can have no effect, that the world is doomed to chaotic violence in spite of our best efforts, does not hold up to scrutiny (and there will be more scrutiny applied in the following pages). The cynical assumption that hope and experience are necessarily adversaries does not fare well, either, though it is a popular narrative.

---

[9]...though arguably less violence than ever before. Steven Pinker argues convincingly in *The Better Angels of Our Nature* that violence has been in steady decline across centuries, as well as decades.

Sheltered young people have big dreams, the narrative goes, and then they encounter the world. Once they understand the unspeakable oppression, cruelty, violence, timidity, and selfishness of which human beings are capable, they give up on those dreams. A solid dose of reality cures them of such silliness. They grow out of it.

If that were true, however, then Nelson Mandela, as a well-known purveyor of hope, would have had to be sheltered from the cruelty of the world in order to hold such a worldview. After all, according to the twisted but pervasive logic of the cynics, Mandela would have had to be at best naive to hold such a view, at worst delusional. Perhaps in his twenty-eighth year of prison, reality would have sunk in, but twenty-seven years as a political prisoner of the Apartheid[10] government in South Africa were apparently not enough to convince him that people can be cruel and unjust.

Two weeks ago, I stood with my hands on the bars of Nelson Mandela's prison cell on Robben Island. He slept on the smooth concrete floor for most of his time there, and he and the other political prisoners received less food than the non-political criminals housed elsewhere on the island. The guard dogs kept on the island literally had more space in their private kennels than Mandela had in his cell.

On that same trip, I went to lunch with Father Michael Lapsley, an Anglican priest active in the anti-Apartheid movement. Ethan Vesely-Flad, of Fellowship of Reconciliation, had introduced us, and Father Lapsley took time from his work at the Institute for the Healing of Memories to have a conversation with my friend Dr. Vernon Rose and me. We met at his office, chatted there for a few minutes, then walked a couple of blocks to a local diner.

---

10 With some agitation and urgency, my South African friend Dave Wanless, who was the Director of Communications for the South African Council of Churches under Desmond Tutu, once interrupted a question I was asking him to correct my pronunciation of 'Apartheid'. I was pronouncing it like a German word, with the last syllable rhyming with 'light', but in Afrikaans, the work is pronounced 'Apart-Hate'. Dave was appropriately insistent: "That's important because that's what it was built on: *apartness* and *hate*.

with Father Lapsley and Dr. Rose in Cape Town in 2014

Father Lapsley is a friendly and sharp-witted man. He smiles easily and doesn't hesitate to poke at pretense, playfully challenging my descriptions of what I'm doing as I answered his questions about why I'm in South Africa. After I told him what I'm working on and why, he answered a few of my questions generously.

"There is a perspective that working for change is adolescent," he said. "Some of my colleagues ask 'Are you still doing that?' as though I should have grown out of it by now. Apparently, we should be drinking scotch and analyzing issues, but not doing anything about them."

But there he is, doing the work. And smiling sincerely and amiably as he does so. I don't pretend to know him well, but based on our brief time together, he strikes me as a man at peace and a man of hope. He knows something, after all, about healing.

Father Lapsley moved to South Africa from his native New Zealand in 1973, taking on the chaplaincy of both the White and Black universities in Durban shortly after he arrived. He began to speak out on behalf of students who were being shot, arrested, and tortured. Later, he joined the African National Congress and became a chaplain to that organization.

In 1990, three months after Nelson Mandela was released from prison, Father Lapsley was sent a letter bomb by the security forces of the South African government. That bomb blew off both of his hands and severely damaged one of his eyes as well.

Now he is working with trauma victims worldwide, focusing on victims of the Apartheid regime and United States military veterans, through an organization that he founded, the Institute for the Healing of Memories.[11]

Has he held on to his hope because he doesn't understand the capacity of humans to be cruel and heartless? Losing his hands to his own government's act of terrorism was not sufficient evidence for him to understand?

Hope is not necessarily maintained at the cost of acknowledging the existence of cruelty and organized oppression. Deep hope is the antithesis of naiveté.

Was Gandhi hopeful because he didn't understand what he was up against, having watched people he loved march unarmed, hands down, into the batons of British troops, who struck them down repeatedly? Or Dr. King? Being beaten repeatedly, jailed time after time, having his house firebombed—that was not enough education for him to understand the human capacity for cruelty and evil?

Or could it be that these people have a broader perspective and a deeper understanding? That they understood all along the moral depravity and cruelty that humans can display and their hope is not predicated on denying it? Could it be that those bright lights have an understanding that reaches beyond our own naiveté? That their worldview is grounded in a reality that encompasses the human capacity for unspeakable hatred and violence but responds with a kinetic hope that, rather than denying that darkness, nourishes the other, equally demonstrable reality of the human capacity for healing, reconciliation, generosity, and empathy?

---

11 http://www.healing-memories.org/

We don't need to suffer the dramatic sacrifices that these people have suffered in order to begin to understand what they have tried to teach us. If we have the wisdom to listen to them, we will learn that hope is not necessarily maintained by refusing to acknowledge the existence of cruelty and organized oppression. Deep hope is the antithesis of naiveté.

And yet people of hope, the ones who talk about changing the world and try to do so, are regularly dismissed as being out of touch with reality.

It is not naive to think you can change the world. In fact, it is naive to think that you could possibly be in the world and not change it.

Imagine being in an anti-Apartheid organizing meeting at a U.S. university in the late eighties, when Nelson Mandela was still in jail, the United States government still supported the Apartheid regime, and things looked quite bleak in South Africa.

What if you had stood up and said, "OK, here's what's going to happen: Nelson Mandela will be released from prison, and then about four years later, South Africa will have free and fair elections in which he will be elected president. There will not be retributive genocide of Whites, and though there will still be many serious issues to deal with, South Africa will largely recover economically and politically. It will end up adopting one of the most progressive constitutions in the world, enshrining civil rights as few have done. I think that's what's going to happen."

How would people in that meeting have responded? I imagine they would have laughed you out of the room as a lunatic, idiot, or both. You would have been considered a starry-eyed dreamer.

But who in the room would have been most in touch with reality? Who had the best handle on what would happen in the real world?

As a culture, we have come to a place where we equate

cynicism with realism and hope with naiveté. But that is, well, unrealistic. Reality sometimes *is* hopeful, and we need not defeat ourselves before we start. There is, of course, such a thing as naive optimism, but living in hope is something altogether different.

Neither is it naive to think that we can change the world. 'Change', remember, is not equivalent to 'fix'.

If we are talking about *fixing* the world—eliminating all conflict, strife, and injustice—then some eye rolling is unquestionably in order. But it is not naive to think you can *change* the world.

In fact, it is naive to think that you could possibly be in the world and *not* change it. Everything you do changes the world whether you like it or not. So the questions we must ask ourselves are 'Which changes will we make?', and 'How will we go about making them?'

Narratives
of Change

CHAPTER FOUR

Out of the Blue

The work of the world is common as mud.

— Marge Piercy

Somewhere around 1997, I wandered down to my local music hall, the Grey Eagle.[12] Two guys I knew, Matthew Kahler and Shawn Mullins, had driven up from Atlanta for a concert. They are both great writers and performers, so I didn't want to miss the show.

Neither did the other eleven people who showed up. The Grey Eagle could hold over two hundred people, so twelve was a bit awkward. The sound system and stage lighting seemed sort of silly with such a minimal crowd.

Shawn and Matthew were already seasoned performers in those days, though, with enough years on the road and enough perspective to sincerely appreciate those folks who did come out rather than complain about those who didn't. They did a wise and appropriate thing, and I learned by watching them. They brought their guitars and Matthew's drum down off the stage. They invited us to make a circle of chairs and sat down in the circle with us. Then they played their show, chatting and laughing casually with people between songs and answering questions as they went. They passed me a guitar and I played a song or two as well. In short, they celebrated and nourished the beautiful intimacy of a small gathering, rather than awkwardly pretending it was a large one.

The next time Shawn came to town, as I recall, he came alone in his pickup truck. Or rather, he came with his little dog,

---

12 In those days, the Grey Eagle was still in Black Mountain, North Carolina, where it was born, though it later moved into the nearby, larger city of Asheville. It's a wonderful music room, where I cut my proverbial teeth as a performer. www.thegreyeagle.com

'Roadie' in the passengers' seat, which was how he usually rolled in those days. The crowd may have been a little bit better, but, as is often the case, it was grossly out of proportion to his talent. Shawn is quite a songwriter and deserved a packed house, as the world would soon discover.

I was packing the Grey Eagle in those days, not in proportion to talent, but because it's my own small town and folks support me here. Shawn consistently sold out Eddie's Attic in Decatur, his hometown venue, and my crowds when I went there were hardly packed. So Shawn suggested that we trade opening slots for each other at our home town concert venues so that each of us could be exposed to the other's audience.

We both liked the idea, and we kept in touch on the phone. A few months later he came back to town and opened for me in front of a solid crowd. He was great, as he consistently is; people loved his set and bought lots of CDs.

In fact, a lot of people were starting to discover Shawn's music, including a major radio station in Atlanta where, a few months after opening for me, Shawn was charting with his song "Lullaby". Subsequently, some major record labels took interest in the song. The verses are spoken in Shawn's gravelly, accessible poetry, and the choruses soar with his pure falsetto in a juxtaposition that is hard to resist, not just because it's catchy, but because the whole spectrum of sound and emotion in the song is undeniably authentic.

Not too long after being picked up in Atlanta, the song was at #1 on Billboard's Adult Contemporary Top 40 charts. It spent eight weeks there and also charted in the U.K., Canada, and Australia. I thoroughly enjoyed watching that success emerge. Shawn had worked hard at his craft for years, and it was a joy to see that paying off.

I never did get in touch to say so, though, knowing that for a while, at least, Shawn would have a whole lot of people trying to get a bit closer. I didn't want to be one of the many people who suddenly wanted to claim him as a best friend. Besides, I didn't want him to feel obligated to thank me, since naturally, I chalked most of his success up to opening for me in Black Mountain. That had to be the tipping point, right?

Sure enough, life quickly became very busy for Shawn, and, by his own description when we talked about it recently, somewhat surreal. He was flying to New York to appear on television talk shows and playing concert venues like Madison Square Garden instead of opening for me in Black Mountain.

One night Shawn found himself sitting in the interview chair with Jay Leno on the Tonight Show. Jay opened the interview by saying something along the lines of, "Wow, you came out of nowhere!"

Shawn smiled good-naturedly and said, "Yeah, I guess after ten years on the road, I'm an overnight success." As Shawn recounted it to me, Mr. Leno was surprised and intrigued by his response, and Shawn had the opportunity to gently challenge the 'overnight success' narrative that we love so much as a nation.

By the time "Lullaby" hit the pop charts, Shawn had been on the road for years. He had studied music formally, led a military band while he was in the service, performed hundreds of concerts, and put out eight independent CDs. That's not overnight.

Shawn's story, however, doesn't fit the narrative we love. As a culture, we prefer the idea that talented artists are 'discovered' and plucked out of obscurity to become stars, somehow skipping over the steady, long-term work of building something valuable. It rarely happens that way, but this idea holds so much more appeal than the truth because it means we might wake up tomorrow and find that we are being celebrated by the nation.

We love to apply the same narrative to our social justice heroes, but it's not true of them either.

> As a culture, we prefer the idea that talented artists are 'discovered' and plucked out of obscurity to become stars, somehow skipping over the steady, long-term work of building something valuable.

1957 FOR comic book

Civil Rights hero and U.S. Congressman John Lewis did not start out being beaten into a coma on the Edmund Pettus bridge. He started out going to a meeting. A representative of the Fellowship of Reconciliation (FOR) was in town to put on a workshop at a church near Lewis' college, and he went to check it out. FOR had recently published a comic book about Dr. King and the emerging Civil Rights Movement called *Martin Luther King and the Montgomery Story*[13], and Lewis was among many students across the South who had read it. He showed up at the meeting with seven or eight other students and listened to a man named James Lawson lead a discussion about non-violent resistance. Lewis and his fellow students were hooked.

They began meeting every Tuesday night to study justice issues and non-violence, from the fall of 1958 into the fall of 1959. As time went on, they practiced role plays of non-violent resistance, abusing each other physically and verbally in order to feel the full weight of what they were up against and prepare themselves to respond nonviolently. Finally, after a full year of study and preparation, they formed the Nashville Student Movement,

---

[13] This classic publication has been republished by FOR, and has been translated into many languages and has been influential in modern nonviolent movements as well. For more information, visit http://forusa.org/mlkcomic

which orchestrated the sit-ins that desegregated Nashville's lunch counters, then movie theaters, then restaurants.

Most people in the United States only became aware of that movement when the sit-ins and the the subsequent violent responses to them suddenly dominated the nightly news. It started, though, with attending a meeting. Or maybe one could argue that it started much earlier than that, when John Lewis heard Rev. King preaching on the radio, or read that comic book. At any rate, it started small.

And for so many people, it stays small and undramatic. And yet these people are the ones who drive the movement and bring about the change. Going to a meeting is not necessarily a 'gateway' action. It may lead to... well, going to more meetings, writing some letters, and talking with some people; and those undramatic actions may matter a great deal in bringing about the changes you seek.

The dozen of us who were at Shawn and Matthew's show at the Grey Eagle won't forget it. That mattered. It moved us and changed us, and it taught me how to approach and honor a smaller-than-hoped-for audience. It wasn't Madison Square, but it wasn't insignificant either.

You may be called to make great sacrifices for things you believe in or you may not, but don't fall into the illusion that what you are doing today has to be grand and heroic in order to matter. Don't discount the value of beginning. It doesn't often come out of the blue. It doesn't have to happen overnight. In fact, I don't know of a time when it ever has.

CHAPTER FIVE

Heroes and Movements

Don't call me a saint. I don't want to be dismissed that easily.

— Dorothy Day

Growing up in the seventies, I had brown corduroy pants, a black and white TV in the living room, feathered hair, and a Trapper Keeper notebook. The widespread cultural turmoil of the Civil Rights Era had subsided, and, other than the occasional school bully and a vague concern that nuclear annihilation might come any day, the cultural space I inhabited felt fairly calm and predictable.

I was born three weeks to the day after Martin Luther King, Jr. was killed. By the time I entered middle school, it had been a generation since Rosa Parks had been arrested. Her story had seasoned enough to feel safe for textbooks. Mrs. Parks was held up as a hero: a seemingly powerless little old African American lady who had made a spontaneous decision not to give up her seat to a White man on a Montgomery bus in 1955 and literally changed the world with her courage.

I was inspired by her story, as I still am, but the shape of that inspiration has changed fundamentally. What I didn't know as a young student is that the version I was being taught had left out or glossed over much of the truth—what I believe to be some of the most important parts.

To begin with, Rosa Parks was hardly a 'little old lady'. On Dec. 1, 1955, the day of her arrest, she was 42 years old. As I write these words, that happens to be the same lens through which I am looking at the world, and I sincerely hope that as you read this, you're offering a hearty 'Amen!' that 42 is not terribly old.

Of course, it may well be that I would have seen 42 as fairly ancient through the big eyes of a young boy. I'm not sure it has tremendous significance anyway, except that it seems to reinforce the perception of her spontaneous rise from helplessness to heroism.

There are other details that are interesting as well, like the fact that Mrs. Parks had quite a bit of Native American heritage, and White ancestry as well. Like my own grandmother, also named Rosa, she had long wavy hair that she only let down at home, pinning it up in elaborate braids and buns whenever she left the house. Without doing anything at all, her very identity challenged the false idea that 'races' can be neatly categorized and separated.

Rosa Parks was not arrested for refusing to stand up so that a White man could have her seat. It's worse than that.

Many other facts are frequently left out of the story, as well, removing painful details of this degrading, systematic oppression. I won't spend a lot of time on them here, but one is worth mentioning: Rosa Parks was not arrested for refusing to stand up so that a White man could have her seat. It's worse than that. Rosa Parks was arrested for refusing to stand up so that a White man could have three empty seats beside him, sparing him the supposed indignity of sitting *across the aisle* from a Black woman.

There was not a White section and a Black section on a bus in Montgomery in 1955, where each were free to sit. There was a White section, which expanded as more Whites got on. A small sign indicating "Whites only" was moved back, row by row, and the people sitting in that row would need to rise and go stand at the back. The entire row would rise and stand so that, in frequent cases, one White person could sit on that row by himself or herself.

I hope your anger rises a bit at that realization, if it is not one you have encountered before. The truth of that story, it turns out, is even more degrading than many of us were taught. There is, however, a much more important difference between the story I was told and the truth.

No one told me in grade school that Rosa Parks had already been an activist for twelve years by the time she was arrested. She was the secretary for the Montgomery chapter of the NAACP (National Association for the Advancement of Colored People), and she was involved in the Women's Political Council in Montgomery. She was a day in, day out activist for years before the day that wrote her name in the history books, and for years afterwards.

Rosa Parks had also traveled to a training camp at the Highlander Folk School in Tennessee the summer before she was arrested. She spent ten days there taking classes and spending time with legendary activists like Septima Clark and Myles Horton, a co-founder of Highlander. Highlander was a hub of civil rights training, voting rights activism, and other social action training in that era, and it was an extremely important part of the growing Civil Rights Movement. It was at an informal Pete Seeger concert at Highlander that Dr. King first heard the song "We Shall Overcome". This is where Rosa Parks trained a few months before she was arrested.

Mrs. Parks had been extremely active in the struggle for civil rights for years before she was arrested. Her decision was not a spur-of-the-moment revelation or flash of courage, but rather the result of long-considered convictions and years of work, training, and practice. That changes the narrative of her famous stand, or rather, sit, on the bus in Montgomery in significant ways.

For most of us, Rosa Parks' life is one day long—December 1, 1955. As it turns out, though, her arrest was hardly the first decision point in her journey. Nor was it the last contribution she would make.

Though it may not seem so at first glance, this change in the story is extremely important. The two different versions of these events demonstrate the fundamentally different narratives behind two conflicting views about how large-scale social change happens. What's more, these two perspectives give us very different sets of instructions for what to do if we would like to see a change.

I was first introduced to the discrepancies between the

popular, sanitized version of Rosa Parks' first arrest and the more nuanced and complete story by author and activist Paul Loeb in his book *Soul of a Citizen*, and I have continued to learn more about it over the years since I encountered it there. Loeb points to this story as an excellent example of the lengths we will go to in order to support what can be called the *Hero Narrative* of change.

In this narrative, large scale change happens when an extraordinary individual takes dramatic action in a moment of crisis. Then the problem is fixed, the threat is removed, and the credits roll. We love that storyline, as evidenced by the fact that it provides the plot for most of our entertainment, and arguably our history books as well.

The Hero Narrative, as appealing as it may sound, is ultimately false.

There is one problem with the Hero Narrative, however—it is simply not how large-scale change happens. The Hero Narrative, as appealing as it may sound, is ultimately false. I'm not saying that people don't do heroic things, or that they don't matter. They do, and they do, and that is to be celebrated. But they are seldom the ones who address the problems on a large scale. Before I explain what I mean by that, it might be helpful to look at a hero story.

There are many examples of heroic action to choose from, but one of my favorites is Wesley Autrey. In 2007, Autrey was in New York City, where he lives, waiting for a subway train with his two daughters, when a young man near him had an epileptic seizure and fell onto the tracks below. Autrey and another bystander jumped down onto the rails to try to pull him to safety. As they got there, they heard a train coming. The other person who had jumped down made the reasonable decision to clamber back up onto the platform. Autrey, however, eyed the space between the train and the floor, then moved the shaking young man into the space between the rails and and covered him with his own body while several train cars raced over them. The space between the ground and the train was about twelve inches, and when the two were pulled up again, Autrey had grease on his hat from the bottom of the train.

There's no question that what Autrey did was profoundly heroic, self-sacrificing, and admirable. And his actions unquestionably had a big effect on Cameron Hollopeter, the young film student whom Autrey saved. It also warmed the hearts of a lot of other people, nationally and internationally. Autrey was all over the news and talk shows, and he received many gifts of gratitude from both anonymous and well-known benefactors.[14] In 2007 he was listed among *Time* magazine's "100 most influential people in the world".

That's the storyline we prefer. If for no other reason, Autrey can be considered extraordinary for this act alone. Few of us can imagine that we would actually have taken such a risk for a stranger. The dramatic act was in response to an unforeseen crisis, and the threat was removed and problem fixed. That's the heroic mythology of change in spades.

It is not, however, a very good model for *large-scale* change. Before we consider why not, though, we need to look at the other narrative for how change happens.

The competing narrative, what I like to call the Movement Narrative, says that large-scale social change is brought about by movements—many people taking small actions that contribute to a large shift. This is the kind of example that Rosa Parks provides in the larger context of her whole story. She was a daily activist, doing the work of a secretary, with, I suspect, all the heroic drama and excitement that title invokes.

This daily activism continued to inform her choices, as did her experience working on a military base, where she first experienced a largely integrated society. Together, these and other influences inspired her to delve deeper into social justice work, seek further training, and eventually take the dramatic stand that she took on that bus.

---

14 Autrey was wearing a Playboy hat that day, and Playboy sent him a lifetime subscription, as well as a new Jeep. Ellen DeGeneres gave him a Jeep as well.

Rosa Parks did not start with the action we all remember today. She started by getting involved in a small, undramatic way, and she continued to work in those ways for years before and after her moment of fame. She understood that her most important action was not her most famous moment, but the accumulated daily work she did throughout her life.

The problem is that for most of us, heroic stories like Wesley Autrey's and the selectively edited version of Rosa Parks'—not to mention Dr. King's or Gandhi's—are more immobilizing than encouraging. These kinds of heroes seem fundamentally different from us, dramatic and larger-than-life, so the idea of their action being a model for our own doesn't even occur to us. If we ever do consider emulating them, we usually focus on the wrong part; we wonder if we would have the courage to be arrested on that bus, rather than wondering if we can clear the time to go to a meeting about an issue in our community.

> The greatness of our heroes is not rooted in their fundamental nature, it is rooted in an accumulation of small, daily choices.

In fact, comparing ourselves to our heroes feels vaguely arrogant. Why? I think it's because of our internalization of the Hero Narrative. We have bought into the idea that they are a fundamentally different kind of people than we are. We interpret this not just as a question of doing what they did, but of being *the kind of person* they were, or are. To compare ourselves, therefore, is to inflate our own significance. We are normal and flawed. They are *übermenschen*. They are saints.

That's wrong-headed. They are neither. The greatness of our heroes is not rooted in their fundamental nature, it is rooted in an accumulation of small, daily choices.

Paul Loeb articulates this well in his bestseller *Soul of a Citizen*, where I first encountered the idea:

Chief among the obstacles to acting on these impulses [to get involved] is the mistaken belief that anyone who takes a committed public stand, or at least an effective one, has to be a larger-than-life figure—someone with more time, energy, courage, vision or knowledge than a normal person could ever possess. This belief pervades our society, in part because the media tends not to represent heroism as the work of ordinary human beings, which it almost always is.

In this passage Loeb echoes the famed Catholic Worker activist Dorothy Day, who said of herself and her fellow workers, "Don't call me a saint, I don't want to be dismissed that easily." I think this is what she was getting at. If we separate heroes from the rest of us, then their stories don't call us to action; they only call us to marvel and applaud.

I suspect that most of the people we have separated and sainted would consider that the worst possible outcome of their notoriety. They would much rather that we begin by taking on something small and getting involved, as each of them did, than that we be awed into immobility.

In an interview with the *New York Times*, Wesley Autrey said "I don't feel like I did something spectacular; I just saw someone who needed help. I did what I felt was right." In George W. Bush's 2007 State of the Union Address, he praised Autrey, saying "He insists he's not a hero."

But doesn't the denial of *being* a hero point back to how ingrained the hero myth is? We know that heroes are 'special' people, set apart, and we know that we are 'normal' people with normal capacities. "I'm not a hero," our hero says in the very moment that there is clear evidence to the contrary, "I'm just a normal person. I just did what I had to do."

It might make more sense to define heroes as 'people who do heroic things', but that's not the definition we actually use. This idea that heroes are defined by their fundamental nature— their difference from the rest of us, their extraordinariness, rather than their choices and actions—is the first point in the definition of the Hero Narrative. Implied in the denial of being a hero is this syllogism: "Heroes are special. I'm not special; I'm normal. Therefore, I'm not a hero."

That piece of dubious logic is followed by the next: "Heroes make a difference. I'm not a hero. Therefore, I can't make a difference."

But the problems with the Hero Narrative don't stop there. Even if you can imagine yourself as a hero, and we assume that heroism is what has a significant effect, how do you display your heroism in order to effect change? Where will you find your oncoming train and student in distress?

This is the Hero Narrative, in a nutshell:

Things change when someone *extraordinary* encounters a moment of *crisis* and does something *dramatic*.

It has three significant elements. The first is that there is something inherently special about the hero. They are extra-ordinary, not ordinary. The second is that there is a moment of crisis. The third is that they respond with dramatic action. It is not the product of ongoing small efforts; it is a moment of quick and extreme decisions in response to an urgent situation that arises without our agency.

Most of us, without ever examining it, subconsciously subscribe to the Hero Narrative. The story is deep in our cultural context. It is the plot to many if not most of our movies. And not just Bruce Willis movies, not just *X-Men* and *Thor*, but *Harry Potter*, *Frozen*, and *Cars II*. This is a central story for us, from childhood on.

The fact that this narrative is ubiquitous and deeply woven into our cultural consciousness combines with the fact that it is false to create a dangerous and dysfunctional pattern. The Hero Narrative is a rotten model for addressing the problems we see. If we draw guidance for our actions from the stories we believe about how the world works (and I believe we do), then this is one story we may need to reconsider.

If we subscribe to the hero myth and we want to have a positive impact, then our instructions can be summed up like this:

Step One:
Wait.

Wait for the hero. You're not a hero, are you? I'm not. We all wake up in the morning and smell our own breath. We know we're not superhuman. We are normal. In fact, most of us constitute our own definitions of the word 'normal'. We are our own baseline.

And even if you can find a hero, or you are part of the small percentage of humanity who could perceive *yourself* as a hero, then what are your next instructions?

Step Two:
Wait.

Wait for the crisis. Then summon all your courage and take dramatic action. Wait and watch for the right moment, when the train is coming or the bus driver asks you to give up your seat, or someone external to you presents a situation that calls forth your courage.

This is a fundamental problem with the Hero Narrative: it is *reactive* rather than *proactive*. That's not extremely effective.

Step Three:

There is no step three because we end up waiting forever for the hero and the crisis to emerge. A very rare few of us may, like Wesley Autrey, find ourselves in a moment of crisis and summon the bravery to do something heroic, and that's wonderful. But is it a useful model for change?

One significant problem with that model is that it denies agency; it emphasizes what happens to you and deemphasizes your ability to examine your situation and make intentional choices about how best to engage in the absence of a crisis.

Subscribing to the Hero Narrative of change can easily make us feel like a little boy at Halloween in his Superman costume, waiting on the porch for someone to cry out in distress so that he can save them. And waiting. And waiting. Finally, he gives up and goes to play some other game, which may be a fair metaphor for what many of us do.

If, however, we subscribe to the movement model, then the instructions are quite different. I'm going to talk more about more bite-sized pieces of that instruction manual later in the book, but it mostly comes down to this: get to work. Find your community and lay out an achievable plan together. Do something small to start with. Bite off a chewable piece and start chewing.

The Hero Narrative is so deeply ingrained in our cultural psyche that we don't even realize it's there, and we've built quite a few castles on its bad foundation. I doubt that the various people who gradually edited Rosa Parks' story down so that it fit the hero myth, in spite of a great deal of evidence to the contrary, were doing so consciously. I suspect they were just trying to tell the story well and dramatically, and so they made it conform to our underlying narrative, a story we love—that heroes are extraordinary people who respond to a crisis with dramatic and unpremeditated action.

That myth also informed an article I read online a few years ago. The title of the article was rather cynical, and I should have resisted the temptation to click on it, but my curiosity got the better of me. It was called "The 8 Most Overrated People in History."

I was surprised and interested to find the nonviolent Indian independence hero M.K. Gandhi on the list. Having studied Gandhi fairly extensively and worked in India with people who knew and worked with him, I found his inclusion intriguing and surprising.

The author's argument, in short, is that, "[Gandhi] was a figurehead for the cause, while various other leaders were doing most of the work," and that, "the Indian independence movement was a strong force well before Gandhi entered the scene."

Through one lens, the author of this article is not so far from the truth. Yes, a lot of others did the vast majority of the work in the Indian independence movement, and they had certainly done a lot of work before Gandhi became involved.

The important part of this accusation, though, is that Gandhi was just a figurehead, while others were doing most of the work. For the sake of argument, let's say that is an accurate portrayal.

Even if we accept that, what is the other alternative? Is the author seriously suggesting that in order to be a real hero Gandhi should have expelled the British Empire from India single-handedly?

Isn't that the implication?

That's what the Hero Narrative would require. A *real* hero would have taken care of the problem himself, this argument implies. It's certainly what a Bruce Willis character would have done.

Is the author seriously suggesting that in order to be a real hero Gandhi should have expelled the British Empire from India single-handedly?

But in the real world, real leaders *lead others* to join them in their work, including those who will become the next generation of leaders. That, I believe, is the true function of heroes: to inspire others. And when a lot of people move a little bit, the problems begin to be addressed.

This means two things. First, it means that the contributions of followers matter a great deal. But second, it also means that we may be fundamentally misunderstanding the job of a leader.

Despite what the Hero Narrative teaches us, our leaders and heroes are seldom, if ever, the ones to actually fix things when the problems are large-scale. Rather, they inspire many others to get involved and address the problem together. In the real world, that's how things change.

The arguments made in this article are deeply rooted in the Hero Narrative. If, however, we understand the true function of a hero, then we find ourselves feeling grateful for the inspiration

Gandhi provided, rather than being offended that his story got a lot of attention.

What effect did Rosa Parks' arrest actually have? The arrest *on its own* meant little. Several others had been arrested in similar circumstances in Montgomery before her. Her arrest had three huge and overarching effects, though, all of which are interwoven.

First, it provided a test case for the court system. Second, it served as the catalyst for a one-day bus boycott, which was so successful that it turned into a boycott that was kept up for over a year.

That, I believe, is the true function of heroes: to inspire others. And when a lot of people move a little bit, the problems begin to be addressed.

The last reason is perhaps the most important: Rosa Parks' arrest was widely publicized. Much of the nation saw it on the evening news. Here was a diminutive, dignified, well-dressed Black woman standing between two large White police officers, being arrested. "Why?", we asked. The answer was that she was being prosecuted for not giving up a seat that she had paid for on a public bus.

Across the nation, there was a small shift. Many people were forced to examine and re-evaluate previously held assumptions about 'the way things are'. It didn't fix the problem, but it did shift things slightly and significantly, and the flames of the Civil Rights Movement in the United States were fanned.

Rosa Parks seemed to agree that her own action was not the most significant part of what happened that day. "At the time I was arrested I had no idea it would turn into this," she wrote. "It was just a day like any other day. The only thing that made it significant was that the masses of the people joined in."

Leaders and heroes can be extremely important, but their importance lies in their ability to inspire and challenge the rest of us, not in their ability to directly right the wrongs.

In fact, heroic figures and charismatic leaders are not always necessary for change, as demonstrated by the Egyptian chapter of the Arab Awakening (known in much of the world as the Arab Spring), where a coalition of activist groups overthrew the Mubarak regime through non-violent resistance. A leader without a movement is ineffectual. A movement without a charismatic, uniting leader is rare, but can still be effective.

One could make the counter-argument that it is moneyed powers, not movements, that really change things. Certainly it would be ridiculous to deny that top-down power and financial resources are strong tools. Clearly, they are. They are not the only kinds of power, however; and bottom-up, grassroots nonviolence can and often does defeat them, even in the face of formidable obstacles. Just between the years of 2000 and 2006, organized non-violent civilian movements successfully challenged entrenched power in Serbia, Madagascar, Georgia, Ukraine, Lebanon and Nepal.

Movements don't need lots of leaders; they need lots of participants.

Even top-down power depends on the cooperation of the masses. Étienne de la Boétie, a young 16th-century political theorist asked in a treatise he wrote as a law student, "Obviously there is no need of fighting to overcome this single tyrant, for he is automatically defeated if the country refuses consent to its own enslavement." He has a point there, one that was picked up by many political theorists after him, including Robespierre, and later, the drafters of the United States Declaration of Independence. The top-down power is always predicated on the bottom-up power. If well-organized and committed, the latter eventually wins.

Still, the Hero Narrative is deep in us, in spite of the fact that it is demonstrably untrue. It informs many of the self-defeating voices in our heads, the ones that ask, "What difference could my tiny efforts make in the face of such a huge problem?"

In fact, those small efforts are the best shot we have at having a large impact. They are the best way to begin addressing a problem. Though the charge against such small actions is that they don't matter, it turns out that the exact opposite is true: they are the most pragmatic approach we can take.

If we cling to the myth that large scale change is effected by dramatic heroic actions, we risk missing opportunities for real impact. As it turns out, movements are more effective than heroes. And movements don't need lots of leaders; they need lots of participants. In the end, the real power lies with us: normal people making small decisions to engage.

CHAPTER SIX

Small Change

We get to be a ripple in the water.

— The Indigo Girls, "Perfect World"

So we know what happened after Rosa Parks was arrested. The history books tell us that a group of pastors met the following evening at Dexter Avenue Baptist Church, and the Montgomery Improvement Association was formed four days later at Mt. Zion AME Church. They elected a young Rev. Dr. Martin Luther King, Jr. to be the president, apparently, as Rosa Parks wrote in her autobiography, because "he was so new to Montgomery and to civil rights work that he hadn't been there long enough to make any strong friends or enemies." We know that position launched him to national prominence and that these events combined ignited the Civil Rights Movement (though, of course, that work had been going on for generations). We know that Rosa Parks became an icon of courage and that foundational changes came to the United States in the wake of her actions.

Now I want to look in the other direction on the timeline of Mrs. Parks' life. As I mentioned before, she was trained in non-violent activism at the Highlander Center the summer before she was first arrested in 1955. We know that she had worked for the Montgomery NAACP as its secretary since 1943. History also tells us that she married her husband Raymond Parks in 1935 and that he was already involved with anti-racism activism when they married.

It is interesting to me that for eight years Raymond went to organizing meetings about race issues and Rosa stayed home. Apparently, Raymond Parks discouraged his wife from going to NAACP meetings because he said it was too dangerous. When she finally did go, however, she got involved quickly, though her stated reason for doing so may make us cringe, looking back from our current cultural context. "I was the only woman there, and they said they needed a secretary," she wrote in her autobiography, "and I was too timid to say no."

I can't help but wonder, though, who invited Raymond Parks to *his* first meeting. That bit of information is lost to time, but I like to imagine the conversation between Ray and Chuck, the friend I've created for him, going something like this:

Chuck: Ray, what are you doing Wednesday night?
Ray: I don't know.
Chuck: I think you should come over to my house for a meeting.
Ray: Maybe. I've got some stuff to do around the house.
Chuck: I'm bringing some of Bonnie's pecan pie.
Ray: Really? All right, I'll be there.

Granted, that is entirely fabricated, but isn't it possible that the initial conversation went something like that? Even if it was more dramatic than that—a passionate appeal to get involved based with manifest injustices argued compellingly by one friend to another—it was still very likely a conversation between two friends that got Raymond Parks to that meeting. And I kind of like the pecan pie story. We don't know for sure, but it could have been that small of a factor.

I don't mean to play too lightly with the very serious risks that Raymond Parks and others were taking by working against racism. Their lives were on the line. But I do find that even in the midst of dramatic and dangerous times, small details and human conversations are often hugely significant.

Looking at my own life, I see many corners on my own trajectory, times when I was headed one way but ended up taking a turn in another direction, that hinge on such small influences. My decision to pursue music professionally rather than focus on mediation, for instance, or meeting and later marrying my wife, or choosing to invite my son Mason into the world after wrestling for some time with whether or not we wanted to have children. Each of those decisions hinged on small conversations or other influences, most of which seemed quite inconsequential at the time.

In the summer of 1987, I was working in Montreat, North Carolina, for the conference center there. In those days they brought in about 100 college students each summer to help run the place (it is many more than that now), and I was hired to run the Audio-Visual crew.

In my free time, I liked to hang around with some of the older staffers who had a band. It changed names and personnel a bit each year, but that particular summer, Will Nash, Bill Graham, Patrick Miller, and sometimes Wade Powell made up the band. Even though I wasn't really a good enough guitar player to be in the band, they were kind enough to occasionally let me sit in on a song or two. I admired them all greatly, and I still do.

One night they let me play a few songs while they took their set break at the Town Pump, a local watering hole in Black Mountain. I plugged in my acoustic guitar, nervous but thrilled, and sang a James Taylor song and a couple of others. While I was playing, Patrick, who was then finishing up a degree in classical guitar performance at the College of Wooster but also played a mean electric, wandered up to stand beside the stage and listen. When I finished my three songs, he cocked his head sideways so his unruly bangs were out of his eyes and said, "That was good, Dave. You could *do* this."

"Do what?"

"I mean, like, do *this.*"

Looking back, it seems like a rather low bar to have set, but at the time I was blown away. Patrick, one of the best guitarists I had ever met, a guy who had the same relationship to cool that Midas had to gold, thought that I was a good enough guitar player and singer to play $2 door gigs in smoky bars to the backs of people's heads while they watched a baseball game at the other end of the bar. That, believe it or not, sounded to me like a dream come true, and it was the first time I had seriously considered the possibility. I went home and did the math: how many shows would I have to do and what would I have to make to realistically support a simple lifestyle?

Many years later, after my music career was established, interviewers have sometimes asked me when I knew I wanted to be a professional musician. I think that's the wrong question. If I ask a hundred 15-year-olds how many of them would like to have their life's work be making up songs and singing them for people, lots of hands will go up. If I then ask them how many of them think that's possible for them personally, however, I get a whole lot fewer hands. I know. I've done it.

The revelation for me wasn't that I wanted to do that, but that it might actually be possible. I had played guitar steadily for five years by the time Patrick dropped that casual comment in the Town Pump, but it opened a door to a life that I hadn't thought was possible. I still had to choose to go through the door and down the road, but that offhand comment pointed the way.

There are analogies to activism in that story. Many of us want to have a positive impact, but we don't get started because it doesn't occur to us that it is actually possible for us—specifically *you*, not 'people'—to have a significant impact.

That story illustrates something else as well. It was such a casual comment for Patrick. I'm sure he didn't remember it a week later. Yet here I am 26 years later, talking about it as a key moment in my life story. It was a small act, encouraging me like that, but it led to an entire career. Certainly there were many other influences that led me into the path I've been walking, but that one mattered. Small efforts very often do.

A cynic might respond by saying, "And they very often don't." That's true too, but it's irrelevant. I am not arguing that all small changes lead to big ones. In my experience, some don't. They just evaporate. What I would forcefully argue, however, is that all big changes are made up of millions of small ones, many of which are determinative; the big change could not have happened without the little one.

One small effort can, and often does, have a huge effect, especially when it is combined with many other small efforts in the same direction. Knowing that leaves me passionate about the value of pursuing small changes, doing the simple things right in front of us. Inviting the friend to the meeting. Nudging someone down a path. Calling the governor's office to weigh in on a bill. Getting a few friends together to talk about how we can have an impact on a given community issue that concerns us. Going to engage the people you're having a problem with. Making a pecan pie.

One of the most important small decisions we make, of course, is where we spend our money. If we are troubled by the fact that much of our clothing is made by sweat shop labor, our twenty-first-century form of slavery, then we can take the trouble to do an internet search on which brands are 'sweat shop free', or buy more of our clothes at thrift shops, or simply buy fewer clothes. If our college or faith community is printing up t-shirts for an event, we can buy them from a company that is committed to ethical labor practices. It's actually not terribly hard, and it makes a huge difference in the lives of the people making those shirts.[15]

I am not arguing that all small changes lead to big ones. In my experience, some don't.

Likewise with investments, it doesn't make much sense to let a company borrow money from you to do things you object to. There are investment brokers who specialize in responsible investing and can customize your portfolio to align with the issues you care about.

My sister Kathy was a heavy smoker for many years, and several attempts to quit had failed. In the end, the tipping point for her was her outrage at cigarette companies intentionally marketing to minors. She decided she simply could not give those companies any more of her money. Where we spend our money is sometimes a small decision, but small decisions very often add up.

---

[15] For more information on sweat shop free products, sweatfreeshop.com is a good place to start.

You may make small efforts to resist (or at least refuse to support) something you object to, or you may make positive efforts to support something you *do* believe in. In both cases, the small change can be hugely significant. The illustrations for this are as myriad as the people doing the work, but one of my favorites is the story of Jo Ann Robinson, another hero of the Montgomery bus boycott, but one we hear much less about than Rosa Parks.

Mrs. Parks was arrested on a Thursday evening, on her way home from work. The news spread quickly through the Black community, and that evening, an attorney named Fred Gray returned a call from Jo Ann Robinson and she told him of Mrs. Parks' arrest. They discussed how best to respond, and the two of them agreed that the Women's Political Council should call for a one-day bus boycott. By midnight, Jo Ann Robinson and two of the students she taught at Alabama State University were printing flyers. On an old school mimeograph machine, they ran 52,500 copies of a flyer (17,500 sheets of paper, three to a page) calling for Montgomery's Black community to stay off of the buses on Monday.

Ms. Robinson and the two students ran copies until 4 AM and strategized about distribution until 7AM; then she went to teach her 8AM class. The flyers were spread all over town through the network of the Montgomery Women's Political Council. Local ministers had a meeting on Friday morning and got behind the boycott as well. In church on Sunday morning, the Black community was again informed of the boycott and encouraged to participate.

As important as that all-night printing sprint was, it was only another chapter in the work Jo Ann Robinson had been doing for years as a leader in the Women's Political Council of Montgomery. The Council had networks in place that provided structure for organizing the boycott once the decision was made. They had actually been planning a boycott for some time already, but had not yet chosen a time to launch it. Rosa Parks' arrest provided the catalyst, but the plans and the framework had already been developed. It is hard to imagine that the boycott could have been so successful if that had not been the case. I suspect that there was very little that could be considered dramatic in that behind-the-scenes work, and there were many, many people involved whose small contributions have been forgotten, but they were essential.

The problems we face as communities, as a nation, and as a world are inarguably daunting. But as individuals, we need to scale our thinking down, at least at first, so that we can take action. Rosa Parks didn't decide to go to jail in 1943. She decided to go to a meeting. Then she decided to help out. Even before her arrest, her work was essential to the movement, just as the work of Jo Ann Robinson and the Women's Political Council was. And what of the two students who helped run those copies? They occupy a significant place in history, but I can't find their names written down anywhere. All we know is that they were young men who were enrolled in the class Jo Ann Robinson taught that Friday morning.

Rosa Parks' arrest provided the catalyst, but the plans and the framework had already been developed.

But there's more. Not only did Rosa Parks do years of day-to-day work for the cause *before* she was arrested; she immediately went back to that work afterwards. Many people will recognize a photograph of her being fingerprinted. When I search the internet for 'Rosa Parks arrest', it is the first image that comes up on the screen.

What many people do not know is that this photograph is not from her arrest for refusing to give up her seat but from a subsequent arrest in February, 1956 when 115 boycott leaders were arrested after the boycott was deemed illegal under Alabama State Law.

While the boycott was going on, people who were participating still had to get to work, so the organizers of the boycott purchased and accepted donations of six station wagons. They also organized 325 private citizens to help with transportation

Rosa Parks' second arrest, February 22, 1956. AP Photo/Gene Herrick

and worked with the local Black taxis to ensure that everyone had a ride to work. Mrs. Parks volunteered as a dispatcher, answering the phone and organizing pick-ups and drop-offs for boycotters. It is her arrest for that work that was captured in this photograph.

The moral of this story is not that the day-to-day work she had done before her arrest mattered because it led her to that famous day, which *really* mattered. Rosa Parks, it seems to me, understood that her most important work *was* the day-to-day work she did, rather than the much-publicized moment for which she is remembered. She put most of her energy into that work for years before and after her celebrated arrest.

We are often immobilized by the enormity of problems we face. We sit still because we can't imagine doing anything on a large enough scale to have a meaningful impact. We think that large problems demand large efforts at correction, and that's true. But we forget that those large efforts are almost always made up of millions of small efforts. Perhaps *your* small contribution is essential to a large-scale change.

I received a small package in the mail one day, a couple of weeks after a workshop I led at a conference in North Carolina. One youth group that had attended had come up with a new motto on the way home in the van and had made up some t-shirts that sum it up pretty well. The shirts read, "Be the pecan pie you wish to see in the world."

CHAPTER SEVEN

The Flawed Hero

The sailor cannot see the north,
but knows the needle can.

—Emily Dickinson

I'm writing today in a setting that is strange for me: a roomy seat in the first class cabin of a US Airways flight to Dallas, Texas. I'll be performing tonight and speaking tomorrow in the towns of Edom and Tyler, and I'm looking forward to that time. Though I've been traveling almost constantly for more than twenty years now and have seen a great deal of the planet, I think this is only the second time in my life that I've flown first class.

Today's luxury is due to an airline pricing anomaly. Because I have to fly with my guitar, pedal box, and various other bits of gear, I need to check two bags. USAirways was offering an upgrade special for one hundred dollars, which means it was cheaper to buy the upgrade than to pay for my baggage. Life is pretty good up here, though the flight attendant clearly spots me as a stranger and kindly keeps explaining various things.

As I loaded my guitar and suitcase into the car this morning in Chapel Hill, a light rain was falling. I was grateful for my Aussie hat and a hand-me-down rain jacket that had once belonged to my wife, Deanna. We sent it to the thrift shop when she no longer needed it, and my mother bought it for me later, not knowing that Deanna had once owned it. It serves me well, and I'm glad it came back to us.

It was a gray and cool morning, uncharacteristically early for that kind of weather in central North Carolina, and if I had said, "What a beautiful sunny day!" to my son Mason, it would doubtless have confirmed some of his concerns about his dad's mental stability; it was clearly grim and drizzly. I often think that this is how many people perceive peace activists—somewhat delusional, living in some pollyanna world where black is white, rain is sun, and despair is hope.

As our plane took off, though, we bumped up through the clouds and suddenly there *was* bright sunshine and blue sky. The plane was more or less right above the house we rent in Chapel Hill when it broke through the clouds, and there it was: a clear, sunny day. It's shocking after the weighty gray of the morning. I'm still looking out the window at that sunshine now.

It doesn't make the rain a lie. It's still a soggy day at my house; I got soaked packing the car. But the sunshine isn't a lie either, and I haven't traveled very far. Both are true; both are present and real, though only one was visible from my driveway.

We get ourselves in trouble with Manichaean thought—either/or dichotomies—and we especially like to apply such thought to heroes. We love to build our heroes up as people without flaws, and then, when we inevitably discover that they *do* have flaws, we love to tear them down again.

This always surprises me. As people with first-hand experience of what it means to be human beings, we ought to have a bit more insight than that. Our own decision-making is flawed and our self-centered natures are certainly manifest, but that doesn't mean we don't have noble motivations as well. As it turns out, all of our motivations are mixed, and all of us are complicated creatures.

Human purity is virtually unknown, and I personally believe it's rather over-rated as a goal. I am all in favor of aiming for growth, but purity is unachievable, and over-emphasizing it sets us up for failure. The problem, conceptually and practically, is that because we assign purity to some individuals and not others, we have the capacity to do two things:

The first is discussed in the last chapter: We can categorize some people—'heroes'—as fundamentally different from ourselves by stripping them of their human frailty. We can't be motivated by their examples because we can't compare ourselves to such noble beings. We then excuse ourselves from any responsibility for action because we deny any similarity between our heroes and ourselves. It is virtually impossible to relate to their moral purity and what seems to be their inevitable destiny for greatness.

Given that tendency, we might expect that once their moral flaws and incapacities are revealed, we would reconsider that fundamental difference between ourselves and our heroes and perhaps wonder if we, flawed as we are, might be called to take some kind of action as well. Unfortunately, that's usually not the way it goes.

Instead, we switch to the second problem with lionizing our heroes: once their frailties and failures are exposed, we dismiss their efforts as hypocritical and disparage any good they might have done as hollow and duplicitous. We point to Dr. King's alleged affairs or Gandhi's legendary temper, and say, "Some peacemakers they were!"

> We love to build our heroes up as people without flaws, and then, when we inevitably discover that they do have flaws, we love to tear them down again.

That allows us to sit still as well, since those do-gooders seem to be up to no good after all. "They're all a bunch of hypocrites and charlatans!" we say, "What's the point?" We might even go further and argue that all people are fundamentally malicious and self-serving, as our broken heroes demonstrate. And if people are fundamentally broken, then why should we try to make any sort of change for good?

So we have it both ways and manage to get ourselves off the hook by switching our logic midstream. Whether we see our heroes as perfect or flawed, we have developed easy rationalizations to excuse ourselves from any kind of responsibility to join them in their work, or to take up work of our own.

I don't think it's that simple. The truth isn't that human nature is fundamentally good or altruistic, nor that it is fundamentally selfish and evil. We are neither good nor bad; we are multifaceted and malleable. Aleksandr Solzhenitsyn got it right when he said, "The line dividing good and evil cuts through the heart of every human being."

My five-year-old son lives in a world of good guys and bad guys, which is developmentally appropriate. As we grow older, however, we need to move past that paradigm, and many of us fail to do so. The result is often that we are kept from actively addressing problems we see because we are so keenly aware of our own failings, so we think we are disqualified.

We don't have to wait until we are pure, until we measure up to some ideal hero (who likely did not measure up to their idealized selves either), before we act. We can take action now, imperfectly. We can honor the imperfection of the efforts of those around us and stop wasting precious energy on judgment, of them and of ourselves.

> I have often heard people say, 'World peace begins by finding peace within oneself.' It may begin there. But it certainly doesn't end there.

I have often heard people say, "World peace begins by finding peace within oneself." There is undoubtedly some truth to that. It may begin there. But it certainly doesn't end there. If we wait to be outwardly active until we are inwardly self-actualized, we will wait forever. It is as foolish to hold ourselves to standards of perfection as it is to hold our heroes to them.

And as for me, I've got a confession to make. I could really get used to flying first class.

CHAPTER EIGHT

Paved with Good Intentions

*The line dividing good and evil cuts through
the heart of every human being.*

— Aleksandr Solzhenitsyn

The other time in my life that I flew first class, ironically, was on a trip to Guatemala to work with PEG Partners in extremely impoverished communities with Guatemalans who had ideas and plans for improving their schools. I got bumped up on a full flight on my way to spend time in homes with dirt floors and limited access to clean water, and just in case my own privileged status in the world wasn't made clear enough to me on that trip, the hot towels and real glass for my drink certainly drew the line starkly.

There I was, sitting in a chair in the middle of the sky, suspended in a painful irony. I could have congratulated myself, I suppose, on spending my time and energy doing this work, by which I hope to improve the chances of some underprivileged kids in Guatemala. I didn't have to be there, and that time is costly to me in significant ways.

But I was making that trip by spending not only financial resources, but natural resources as well. Air travel is one of the more destructive habits of the wealthier percentiles of the planet's population, and the money and carbon spent on that plane ticket could arguably have been spent for a better purpose than physically moving me back and forth.

I certainly gain a lot by going to Guatemala, too. It's hard to paint the relationship as pure altruism (nor do I wish to). I have made good friends there, and I enjoy the food and the company and the sometimes breathtaking beauty of the place. I try to make a couple of trips each year to Guatemala, and in the ten years since

Deanna and I founded this non-profit organization, I have spent a great deal of time running it back in the United States. I'm not paid for that work, but PEG does pay for part of my travel expenses, allowing me to spend time with friends in Guatemala without having to shoulder the entire financial burden myself.

It's also good and healthy for me to have the chance to step away from my 'normal' life in order to be reminded of how far from normal it seems to much of the world. There are many definitions of 'normal', and I need occasional reminders of that in order to know who I am and where I fit into the world. Among the many reasons I am grateful for that time in Guatemala is the fact that the occasional shift in perspective helps me understand my responsibilities—what is mine to do.

So am I a hypocrite? Is this self-serving? Is my work in Guatemala a costly exercise in self-congratulation for a privileged do-gooder that ultimately has little real positive impact? Or is it a meaningful contribution?

Is it worthwhile to develop those relationships and work on those very real justice issues in Guatemala, helping to open doors of opportunity for kids there who might not have much of a chance otherwise, and opening myself to challenging perceptions of where I fit into these problems? Is it a responsible action for a U.S. citizen to take, given my own country's role in manipulating governments and perpetuating inequality in Central America for our own economic gain?[16] Is it the best use of my time, passion, and energy to get involved in Guatemala when there are plenty of pressing needs in my own community in North Carolina? Those are questions I've wrestled with for years, and I think it is important to keep wrestling with them because the balance may shift, and I certainly have much more to learn.

My working hypothesis is that most of the above is probably true. It's not one or the other; it's both. I do believe that the positive impact we're having in Guatemala is significant and worthwhile.

---

[16] For a history of how this has played out in Guatemala, I recommend the book Bitter Fruit: The Story of the American Coup in Guatemala by Stephen Schlesinger and Stephen Kinzer.

Through partnerships with other excellent organizations like Child-Aid and LEAF International, we are reaching thousands of Guatemalan children and offering not just literacy but also critical thinking skills, which have not traditionally been prevalent in Guatemalan public schools, even among teachers.

Literacy and critical thinking are essential for all of the changes that my Guatemalan friends tell me are needed in their country—political, economic, and social. If someone doubts that we're having an impact, I can introduce them to children whose lives are different, and arguably much better, because of our work. These kids will have more opportunities and more choices because of the higher quality of education and the significantly improved nutrition they are getting because they have a chance to go to school.

I gave a talk at a church last year, and during the question & response session that followed, one woman asked, "Why do you work overseas when there are so many problems right here in the United States? Isn't it easier to go somewhere else than to work in your own community?"

That is a common question and criticism, but I find it troubling for several reasons. First, it assumes that we can only do one or the other. I think both are deeply important, and we are not limited to choosing one. Along with my work in Guatemala, I also work on issues in my own country, in my home state of North Carolina, and in my little town of Black Mountain. I absolutely believe that all of this work matters. What disturbs, me, though, is an undercurrent I sometimes perceive in such a question. If the questioner is saying, "Kids in our community matter too," then I wholeheartedly agree with that statement, and I encourage the person asking the question to work hard for kids in that community, since they bring that passion.

Sometimes, though, I get the feeling that the person asking that question is suggesting that kids in their community matter *more* than kids in other places. Those values are not unusual, but I do not share them. Healthcare activist, doctor, and author Paul Farmer has said, "The idea that some lives matter less is the root of all that is wrong with the world." He may not be far off.

The suggestion that it is easier to work out of the United States than it is to work in our own communities troubles me, too. In some ways it *can* be easier, especially if we don't maintain the relationships we form, but instead simply 'parachute in' without long-term connection and impose our own solutions rather than listening and being guided and instructed by the people who are most directly affected. Accountability and listening are fundamental to worldchanging (I'll discuss that further in the 'Community' chapter of this book).

Paul Farmer has said, "The idea that some lives matter less is the root of all that is wrong with the world." He may not be far off.

In other ways, however, working in another country is often harder; time away from family, material comfort and expense, getting out of one's cultural comfort zone, and sometimes real risk of personal safety are all part of the equation. I work in Guatemala for many reasons, including a sense of indebtedness for my government's destructive role in Guatemala's history, the fact that we can leverage so much impact with much smaller financial investment, and the degree of need, which is quite extreme.

But there are also valid criticisms to be made. A good friend of mine believes that charity work, if it does not also engage in justice work, is destructive because it props up untenable and unjust systems. And she's not just speaking in the abstract. She saw it play out in her own community, where she had a bird's eye view.

Jen (I'll call her) attended a church in a small southern town while she worked during the week as a community organizer and the director of a food bank. Many members of that church supported the food bank, where the poor residents of the town, primarily African American, often came to eat. Jen's church, made up primarily of middle and upper class White people, felt good about its charity, and the poor people in town had food that they needed, though presumably they may not have felt as good about the situation, trading dignity for food.

Most of the people who ate at the food bank worked at the mills in town, which were owned by some of the people Jen went to church with. After she had been there some time, she found herself privy to conversations in which the mill owners complained about government regulations requiring them to improve ventilation in the mill in order to make it safe for the workers, and ways they were trying to get around those regulations in order to avoid the cost. "In addition," she told me, "people from my church had loan companies with 25 percent interest rates that kept people perennially in debt. They donated their used clothes, leftover food, and some money to charity, but they resisted any challenge to the system that perpetuated that poverty."

Over time, Jen came to understand that keeping the mill workers fed at the food bank was maintaining a system of abuse by a company that chose not to pay them enough to eat. They were replacing justice with charity. The soup kitchen served as an enabler to this system as well as a salve to the consciences of her fellow parishioners, and Jen began to feel complicit in this system of abuse.

Back in Guatemala, helping to support public education efforts financially may take some of the heat off of the Guatemalan government to shoulder that responsibility itself. Or at least, not unlike the mill owners at Jen's church, PEG Partners may help myself and others sleep better at night in the face of the many global economic injustices in which we are participating.

Those are important and serious things to consider, and should not be lightly dismissed. As I said when I laid out definitions in an earlier chapter, my own shorthand for the difference between aid and social justice is that aid work is trying to meet people's needs, while social justice work is challenging the systems that make them needy. And though I wish it were not true, I do believe that aid work can sometimes undercut social justice work. Put otherwise, meeting people's short-term needs can undermine systemic changes.

"Right now I'm seeing more charity and mission trips than I have ever seen," Jen wrote to me. "And yet it is rare that these same people question why the charity is needed and what long term change they want to impact. For many of these folks, charity is the end of the line, and the only outcome they think is necessary." Speaking again of the relationship between the food bank and the church, she wrote, "The charity dulled everyone to the injustice of that whole economic system. The people in that church remained adamantly opposed to any and all social justice work."

Jen's growing understanding of the generationally entrenched injustice in her community eventually led her to leave that work and turn her attention to more systemic change, with which she is still involved. She remains understandably skeptical of charity.

The recent books *Toxic Charity* and *When Helping Hurts* both take on various ways in which well-intentioned aid projects can be destructive of dignity, relationships, and opportunities for larger shifts in oppressive systems. Those are important conversations to have, and though I have criticisms of each book, I think both of them offer some good insights.

It seems to me that there are also risks to dwelling on the destructive examples, however, overgeneralizing and dismissing all aid work as destructive, which seems to be a popular stance among some social justice activists (though, I should say, not my friend Jen, who is a nuanced thinker, and has taught me a great deal). There are times when a short-term solution (aid) is needed to get through a crisis, so that we can find our way to a long-term shift toward sustainability (justice).

I include this story because it is real, and sadly not isolated. Hope cannot be predicated on denying hard realities. There is a danger in overextending, however. I also think it is important to acknowledge that not all aid work conforms to this pattern. We need to be careful that valid critiques of charity do not simply end up as rationalization for withdrawing support of projects that could be improved, rather than doing the work of improving them, where that is a tenable possibility.

In the context of PEG's work in Guatemala, it does not seem

wise to sacrifice the education of this generation of children in order to keep up pressure on the government; certainly not when I'm being asked to help and I have a way to do so. I think it is much more likely that facilitating an education and some training in critical thought will allow these children to grow up to challenge injustices in their own society than it is that our work will contribute to maintaining the status quo.[17]

To return to the fable about aid v. social justice earlier in this book, marching the whole team upstream to see who is throwing the babies in the river means that the ones who are coming down now will likely drown.

When we are challenging a flawed model, the primary question we need to ask is whether we are challenging it for the purpose of doing it better or challenging it because it should be discarded. When we see that something is broken, we have the choice to either ask, "How can we make it work better?" or to throw up our hands and say, "It's no use!" Sometimes it really is no use, and we should put our energy elsewhere. But if we give up on aid work on principle, we'll be throwing a lot of babies out with the bathwater ...or maybe river water.

The common criticisms of aid work mostly fall into two categories: one, that it is ineffective, or even destructive, perpetuating oppression; and two, that it is actually self-serving. The first is a question of outcomes, and the second is largely a question of motivation.

Taking my own inventory, there is no question that I feel good about my work with PEG Partners in Guatemala, and that is a benefit for me. So is that primarily why I do it? I can't deny that it is a factor. Of course I want to feel like I'm having a positive impact, and the last decade's work in Guatemala does give me some evidence that I am. I don't think it is the primary reason I'm doing this work, but I can't pretend that it isn't a part of the mix.

There are no absolutes in these conversations. If we remove the nuance, we remove part of the truth. The bottom line for me,

---

17 Happily, there have been some positive shifts in the Guatemalan government's education policy in recent years, and aid projects do not seem to have impeded that.

though, is that all of our efforts as human beings are driven by complicated motivations and have mixed outcomes. We fail not by having impurity within us, but by valuing only purity. If we are to do what is needed, it might be wise of us to spend a bit less energy tearing down our own good efforts, and each other's. Imperfect plans and mixed motivations can reach a point where they are problematic, but I strongly suggest that they are seldom our biggest problem. Apathy and inaction are of far greater concern, and attacking the effectiveness or motivation of good efforts is perhaps our most popular method for justifying our own inaction. Doing good work in the real world is messy and complicated, morally as well as practically.

Attacking the effectiveness or motivation of good efforts is perhaps our most popular method for justifying our own inaction.

The danger of moral absolutism is that it is yet another way to immobilize ourselves and each other. Our imperfections become, ironically, an excuse not to act. We are all hypocrites, in the sense that our actions will never perfectly match our values as we profess them. The question is whether we will be hypocrites who make the world a bit better today or hypocrites who spend our time calling each other hypocrites in order to excuse our own inaction.

In the end, I suppose that realization makes me skeptical of skepticism. It is so often an excuse for inaction.

The morality of any person or effort is open to interpretation. The evidence can be analyzed in many ways, and it seems to me that most of us have a tendency to interpret it to support our preconceived understandings of human nature.

A great deal of ink and air have been spent discussing the fundamental nature of humanity, whether we are essentially good or essentially evil, or perhaps, to put it differently, essentially selfish or essentially cooperative. Those are interesting abstract conversations, and I enjoy them. I have weighed in a bit on those questions already. At some point, though, they simply cease to have much relevance to real problems and efforts to address them.

Both within ourselves and in relationship to the world around us, the question of fundamental moral nature becomes a dead end. The conversation itself becomes paralyzing. We have the capacity both for tremendous good and tremendous harm, for unfathomable generosity and self-sacrifice and for staggering selfishness and cruelty. Most of the time, though, we live neither on one end of the spectrum nor the other. We are a complicated mix of all of it, all in the same moment. And that is as true of our efforts in community as it is of our individual lives.

"First, do no harm," is a popular mantra among some people working for positive change. I don't think it is a realistic one, though. Sometimes even the most successful efforts also do real harm.

And outcomes, though they are somewhat more tangible than motivations, are still difficult to neatly categorize, as hard as we may try. "First, do no harm," is a popular mantra among some people working for positive change. I don't think it is a realistic one, though. Sometimes even the most successful efforts also do real harm.

The United States Civil Rights Movement, for example, decimated Black-owned businesses. African Americans were finally allowed to shop at businesses that were previously only available to Whites, but White customers did not support Black-owned businesses in the same way or to the same degree. So the Civil Rights Movement indisputably did *real harm* to Black-owned businesses. That's not a reason to regret the movement or its achievements, however. It is an invitation to work on the next issues, some of which may arise from the good work that has been done.

We should not be cavalier about harm done, nor minimize it, but we should also be careful not to delude ourselves into thinking that any large-scale change can take place without some real harm. That can easily become one more way to paralyze ourselves.

In any effort for positive change, it is wise to study, plan, consult mentors, and reflect on earlier experience in order to minimize negative consequences. We should try hard to maximize the good impact and minimize the negative. All too often, though, we see complexity and simply quit before we even begin.

We tend to think that if something is good, it will be purely good. Too often, we shake our heads and say, "See? This does damage as well as doing good!" as though this is a rational argument for taking no action.

That's simply not the way the world works. Good work is complicated and may cause damage, but inaction in the face of manifest injustice is simply opting for the harm we know rather than the potential for harm that we can't fully predict.

As it turns out, the adage is true: the road to hell is paved with good intentions. It's not the only road that uses that kind of stone, though. The roads to compassion, community, and positive change are also paved with the stones of good intentions, carefully laid by people who take the time to reflect and be intentional about the final destination and how they intend to get there. The question is, 'Which road will you build?'

CHAPTER NINE

Community

"If you want to go fast, go alone.
If you want to go far, go together."

—African proverb[18]

Until the most recent chapter of history, community was a given. As clown activist Patch Adams writes in his book *House Calls*,

Throughout most of human history, a community was a tribe, and later a village. Initially, community offered protection, safety and insurance against any threats that came along. Today, in the absence of tribal communities, many people must be responsible for their own security. I think that our society's high level of anxiety is mainly due to this loss of belonging.

In the era, country, and neighborhood where I live, community no longer happens automatically. We have to seek it out and create it if we find it to be of value. It is entirely possible to live one's life with very little contact with other people and very little awareness of what binds us together in relationship.

This isn't how it has to be, and it's not the case everywhere. In the places I have travelled that people in the West refer to as 'developing countries'—India, Guatemala, Haiti, and many others—the value of community has remained far more culturally intact. In rural villages in particular, everyone knows everyone else and what

---

[18] 'African proverb' can sound like a dubious attribution, but I encountered these words not only on a poster on the wall of a Zambian pastor's office, but also written in large letters on the wall of the Johannesburg airport in South Africa, so it is legitimate in this case.

they are struggling with or celebrating. They live in the context of deep community. They would think it bizarre not to.

The social isolation that is increasingly prevalent in my own context is also not the norm in all parts of the United States. More private lifestyles are much less common in poor, urban neighborhoods, for instance, where space is at a premium.

In my own middle class White context, our relationships with our own next-door neighbors are often reduced to a mere nodding acquaintance, if we know them at all. It is true that via technology, we are much more connected to people far away from us than we used to be, but those distant relationships often seem more disposable and temporary. It is as easy to unplug from them as it is to plug in. As sociologist John Brueggemann writes in his book *Rich, Free, and Miserable*, "There is a correlation between physical proximity and the 'moral intensity' people feel about a given situation. We tend to be more conscientious when we pay attention to the problems nearby."

This is a significant problem for people living in this more isolated social context, especially if we believe in the Movement Narrative of change, but I would argue that it's not an unsolvable one. We have the capacity to create and develop community, if we value it. If we want to work for positive change, this should be one of our top priorities.

Community has no place in the Hero Narrative, which is one more indication that this narrative is simply not true. If we want to have a positive impact in the world, community is essential. So where is yours? If that question is not easy to answer, perhaps it is better to ask, 'How will you create it?'

Just Get Started

In 2011, on the tenth anniversary of the September 11 attacks, I found myself fighting downtown New York City traffic. I had been invited to lead a remembrance service that morning at a Presbyterian church in Woodbury, New Jersey. It was a difficult but meaningful service; I tried to hold in the same hand the pain and loss that people in that community had suffered—some quite directly—and also questions about how we have responded as a nation in the years since those attacks, and who we wish to become now.

When the service ended, I left all my gear set up, threw one of my guitars into the back of my car, and raced up to New York City for my next show, a concert called 'Love Wins' honoring first responders and trying to make space for healing. New York City had not invited first responders to the official commemoration events of the day, and this event was created as an effort to honor their courage and sacrifices, as well as to offer a more restorative vision of how to move forward.

Though I was feeling the weight of the day's remembrance, I was also admittedly excited. I was on my way to perform with Pete Seeger, David Amram, Spook Handy, and other musicians I greatly admire. I could hardly imagine any better place to mark that day, or better people with whom to do so.

In the months following the 9/11 attacks, my friend Lyndon Harris had headed up the relief efforts based out of St. Paul's Chapel, which stands less than a hundred yards from the World Trade Center site but survived strangely unscathed. As a result, he became something of a national celebrity. With Lyndon's leadership, volunteers turned the sanctuary into a relief center, addressing the physical and emotional needs of the first responders and others working at the site. They provided food, massage, music, counseling, and space for naps on the pews, and made a huge community effort to provide for countless other needs, material, emotional, and spiritual.

Lyndon showed up for his part in the crisis, but after that acute need had subsided, he turned his attention to the ongoing work of healing and forgiveness, not just from this specific instance of mass violence, but from violence all over the world. He established Gardens of Forgiveness, a non-profit organization which works to teach the skills and value of forgiveness and establishes places of refuge for people to contemplate forgiveness as it relates to their own experiences of trauma. There are now Gardens of Forgiveness in Long Island, New York, Charleston, South Carolina, and Beirut,

Lebanon, though the incredibly complicated political context of the World Trade Center site has thus far prevented the original goal of establishing a Garden of Forgiveness there.

That particular day, as I tried to weave my way through the streets of Soho, people were busily setting up the room for the concert a few stories above me. Racing to fit both events into the same day, I actually arrived moments after the concert began, though fortunately well before my slot in the program.

One of the stories that sticks with me from that day is one I was told by my long-time friend Sarah Hipp, who had helped to organize the concert. She told me that, while setting up for the concert, the late and legendary folk singer Pete Seeger came in, took a look at the room, and shook his head. The chairs, which were of the movable cushioned variety, were set in straight rows, forming a large rectangle with an aisle down the middle. As a seasoned organizer, Pete understood that there is nothing straight or rigid about community. If you want to create community, you have to welcome people into it; he wanted the chairs to curve.

> Gandhi did not say, "Demand the change you wish to see in the world." He said, "Be the change you wish to see in the world."

Pete wasn't the kind of musician who expected people to serve as spectators to something he did for them. He wanted them to participate, both in singing the songs and in changing the world. He wanted to create real relationships and alliances and get people involved, not only with him but with each other. In order for that to happen in this concert, people needed to be able to see each other, to curl around each other physically as well as emotionally.

Pete Seeger was a legend, but he was no prima donna. He didn't issue orders or make demands. He didn't ask anyone to change the chairs, or even to help him move the chairs. He just started moving them.

Singing with Pete Seeger in New York on Sept. 11, 2011

At 92 years old, Pete began moving each of the hundreds of chairs, one by one, until they served the community better. He knew well that Gandhi did not say, "Demand the change you wish to see in the world." He said, "*Be* the change you wish to see in the world." Pete perceived a change that he wished to see, so he got to work. He did the same thing with litter, picking it up everywhere he went.

When Sarah expressed some concern for him doing the manual labor of moving those chairs, he responded by saying, "Oh, it's OK. I didn't get to chop wood today." He was not one to sit idly by when there was work to do, and he led by example.

Showing up means more than inserting your body into the situation; it means participating in whatever you show up for, in whatever big or small way may be called for in that place and that moment.

It's not surprising that others in the room noticed what Pete was doing, and he very soon found himself accompanied by a crew of volunteers moving chairs. The job was done quickly, and the event was better for it. Pete Seeger was in the business of creating community, but the way he did it is not by haranguing or cajoling others. He simply began, and people noticed. And because the work he did was so inspiring, people joined in. They wanted to be a part of it, and they wanted to hear more of the story. In the process, they found each other.

Showing up and getting to work is how things get done. It's another narrative that we tend to get backwards. We think that people who have a big impact start out with a great plan, recruit the support team they need, and then implement it. In fact, most of them start out by showing up, beginning, and recruiting and revising as they go.

My brother-in-law Eric, who lives just up the road from me in Asheville, has spent the last year of his life following his nose into things that interest him. He's a computer guy who also has a deep sense of the need for civic engagement. Following those passions, he started connecting with some people in the community who also care about things he cares about, in a group called Code for Asheville. Together, they started meeting with some city government officials as well, and one of the things he realized as he learned more about the city is that it is extremely difficult for most people to figure out what the city government is actually doing. So Eric and some other volunteers created a web site that makes the city budget extremely easy to see, using graphic interfaces and telescoping levels of detail.[19] It gives average citizens a way to be more engaged with their local government and increases transparency, which is good for the whole community. Now he's finding that doing this for other municipalities is his calling. He didn't know that when he started going to meetings, though. He didn't actually know it until last week.

Of course, when we take action, we open ourselves to criticism. Showing up and getting to work is an inherently vulnerable thing to do, whether it takes the form of speaking up in a

---

[19] www.AVLbudget.org/

conversation, going to a workshop, writing a letter to a newspaper, or visiting the folks camping out in the park to protest an injustice. It's how our most meaningful work generally begins, though. We have to decide to show up.

Unexpected Community

In 2003, I went to Big Spring, Texas, at the invitation of a Presbyterian church in the area, to spend a few days leading workshops and having conversations. This is west Texas, spacious, flat, and dusty, and my friend Matt Miles was the pastor there. Matt is also an EMT and a fireman; he's full-on cowboy, complete with boots, tight jeans, pick-up truck, and chewing tobacco. He is also well-versed in that particular brand of sardonic Texas wit that is sharper than a cactus needle.

One of the things we did with that time was hold a workshop on peacemaking. That probably doesn't sound too radical or dangerous in most contexts, but keep in mind that this took place in the early days of the Iraq war, when any concern expressed about whether or not the war was a good idea was often met with angry and serious accusations of treason. These were also the early years after the 9/11 attacks, and the nation as a whole was injured, angry, and prone to lashing out.

Add to that the fact that we were gathering thirty-nine miles up the road from Midland, where George W. Bush spent the early part of his childhood. Big Spring is the former home of Webb Air Force Base and the former headquarters of Cosden Oil. A big refinery remains, but Cosden and Webb are long gone, and both losses have been extremely costly for the town. This was not a town you would think of as being particularly sympathetic to the peace movement.

We had a good conversation, though it was painful in places. There were military veterans there, as well as people with family currently serving in the military. There were plenty present who felt strongly that the Iraq war was necessary and right, and the conversation was occasionally heated.

These people were all trying to do the right thing, though they had wildly divergent perspectives on how to go about it. However, as we continued to talk, people began to feel increasingly comfortable. The conversation wasn't easy, but it was real, and the mood gently shifted as people began to believe that this was a safe space in which to be honest.

Well into our time together, one woman expressed some real reservations about the Iraq war, and later, another did too. The conversation went on for some time after that; I presented some ideas, but mostly, in that setting, my job was to create space for the conversation and ask some constructive questions.

As we closed out, I recall one of those women saying that she was glad to have discovered that the other felt the way she did. Before that, she said, she felt like she was the only one. These two women knew each other, but they had never known that they shared this view, presumably because they had been afraid to speak it. The two of them found each other, and some comfort and inspiration, because they showed up *for* the conversation that day, and then showed up *in* the conversation.

This is another argument for showing up, both literally and metaphorically: it's really the only way we can find each other. It's the only way to create healthy community with a sense of connectedness. And community, as costly and messy as it is, is our best way forward.

What Makes A Community?

Of course, the word *community* is another nebulous bit of vocabulary. We often use the word to refer to our physical neighborhoods or towns. In recent years we have re-defined it to include communities of cause, communities of classification (for instance, 'the LGBT community' or 'the Latino community'), and virtual communities of people who share common interests or goals, yet have never met in person. Regardless, the word community indicates interrelatedness—relationships that are woven between multiple people that provide the context for our actions together.

My friend Hugh Hollowell leads an organization called Love Wins in Raleigh, North Carolina, that nurtures a community that is partly made up of people who are experiencing homelessness. He argues that homelessness is not fundamentally an economic problem but is rather a problem of relationships. If my house burned down tonight, I would not be homeless because there are people in my community, family and friends, who would take me in. Many people who are homeless are without shelter primarily because they have run out of community.

In general, I have been writing in this book about communities of cause: people who are working toward similar goals together. It is important to acknowledge, though, that there will never be a community of human beings who will be completely aligned in their thoughts, values, and approaches. Conflict within communities, though more evident in some than others, is always a part of what it means to work together, and it is very often a good thing.

The two of them found each other, and some comfort and inspiration, because they showed up for the conversation that day, and them showed up in the conversation.

Communities that are not chosen based on agreement, but rather exist through circumstance, such as our neighborhoods or towns—or even our families—are perhaps the most important places for us to work for positive change, and our deepest sources of nourishment and growth when we can create healthy relationships and patterns. When we don't start from an assumption of common interests, we have to work to find them. We will often find that we have at least some common interests, and the process of discovering them can be enriching.

One of the fundamental principles of effective conflict mediation is the need to shift from *positions* to *interests*.

As Roger Fisher and William Ury write in their small and seminal book *Getting To Yes*, "Behind opposed positions lie shared and compatible interests, as well as conflicting ones."

In the peace workshop in Big Spring, Texas, we found that after some solid conversation, people were eventually able to hear each other's concerns, fears, and perspectives more respectfully, even if they still disagreed passionately about the best course to take. Most of the people in the room supported the war in Iraq. A few opposed it. But everyone in the room wanted their families to be safe. Some people had supported their families through income derived from the military, and had a natural allegiance to military orientation and approaches to problems. They may have also held some understandable defensiveness to what they perceived as attacks on the integrity of military leaders whom they admired, including the Commander in Chief. Many of us in the room felt wounded and scared, and some wanted retribution, believing that it might provide some comfort or that it was simply what was right.

One of the fundamental principles of effective conflict mediation is the need to shift from positions to interests.

Others may have had experiences of violence and retribution in their own lives that led them to question whether violence can be a path toward growth and healing. Some may have perceived this latest iteration of violence as part of an ongoing pattern that needed to be stemmed rather than replicated.

Everybody, though, wanted to feel safe, and for some time after the September 11 attacks, very few people in the United States did. I have written a fair amount in this book about the need to humanize our heroes rather than seeing them as 'other', but it is at least as important, if not more so, that we humanize our opponents. That is sometimes an extremely challenging task, especially as we have the increasing opportunity to 'silo' ourselves into social contexts where we mostly encounter only people who think more or less like we do.

When we can manage to actually stop and listen to each others' perspectives, I have frequently seen a shift occur in contentious conversations. We may not convince each other, but we are less dismissive of people with whom we disagree because we understand the interests beneath the positions. If we can articulate, acknowledge and agree on the commonality of some of those interests, we have a productive starting place to move toward meeting them.

In the example from Texas, there were people there who felt unsafe and believed that war in Iraq would make us safer (by eliminating a threat and an enemy and by increasing regional stability through military might). There were also people there who felt unsafe and believed that war in Iraq would make us even less safe (by diverting resources needed elsewhere and generating animosity toward the U.S. that would create more enemies where they didn't exist before, haunting us for decades to come and further destabilizing the region). There were many other reasons people believed that the Iraq war was the right or wrong course of action, but those two make for a useful illustration, since they point to the same goal: being and feeling safe.

Everybody, though, wanted to feel safe, and for some time after the September 11 attacks, very few people in the United States did.

At that point, if we are really listening to each other, we have the opportunity to relate to each other across the lines of the conflict: "I get what you're saying. You love your kids and you want them to be OK. We disagree on how best to achieve that, but I get it."

In doing so, we restore some of each other's humanity and some of our own, whether or not we come to agreement on how best to move forward. Ironically, a small shift like that can make the world feel a bit safer; and that, after all, was the goal in the first place.

Harmony Is Not Homogeneity

Communities of context rather than cause are important. They give us the opportunity to do the work of humanizing people who are different from us in various ways, and may see things through other lenses than we do. The same is true, of course, in communities of cause, where we are among people with whom we largely agree. Seeing the mistakes we make together, adjusting our own perspectives as we learn from each other, and watching others adjust theirs—these small shifts help to subvert the Hero Narrative. Understanding our heroes' humanity can be extremely empowering.

Another deep value of work in community is coming to understand the practical value of diversity. Sadly, the word *diversity* has increasingly been limited in common parlance to mean specifically racial diversity. That is certainly an extremely important kind of diversity, but there are many others. When I begin workshops, I often begin with a 'Diversity Welcome',[20] which acknowledges the various kinds of diversity present in the room. I take a moment to welcome the women in the room. I take a moment to welcome the men. I welcome people who are feeling energized, then people who are feeling weary. Then people who consider themselves leaders. Then people who do not consider themselves to be leaders. People who are gay. People who are straight. People who don't feel like either of those terms applies to them. Then people of faith. Then people who claim no faith. People who feel at home in this group, who are 'from here', or who are deeply involved with the topic. People who are uncomfortable in this group, who consider themselves outsiders, who are just beginning to explore this topic. People with skin the color of a walnut, or of a mocha swirl, or of a cantaloupe. People who consider themselves young. People who no longer consider themselves young. I welcome Republicans and Democrats and people who support other parties, as well as people

---

20 This is a conflict transformation tool I learned and adapted from Training for Change. www.trainingforchange.org

who support no party. Sometimes, I welcome people in each decade of age that is represented.

Depending on the situation, I customize it, but I almost always find it to have a powerful effect. I look people in the eye and take my time with it because I really mean it. Diversity is not just a matter of political correctness. Having different identities, perspectives, and life experiences in the room enriches a gathering, especially when the gathering is for the purpose of discerning a way forward together.

Diversity of perspective and experience can lend depth, richness, and subtlety to our work in the same way that musical notes in harmony can lend depth, richness, and subtlety to music. Harmony has always been a fascinating word to me, since it bridges my lifelong interests in music and peace work.

Just as with music, notes sung or played in unison are simply not as rich as the combination of many different notes singing or playing in harmony.

As a synonym for *peace*, however, I think that harmony is often misunderstood. It cannot, by definition, mean homogeneity. That's unison, not harmony. And just as with music, notes sung or played in unison are simply not as rich as the combination of many different notes singing or playing in harmony. We need diversity for that.

Of course, it is also true that many notes playing together may clearly *not* be in harmony with one another. Creating that confluence takes intention, patience, and work. It is a beautiful thing when we achieve it, though. And it is not achieved by eliminating difference, but instead by finding ways to work together that are mutually nourishing, that honor and reveal each others' gifts.

We have better ideas in community, too, though many of us are resistant to that idea, whether consciously or unconsciously.

In their insightful book *Switch: How to Change Things When*

Change Is Hard, Chip and Dan Heath cite a fascinating study in which a group of people was asked to generate and consider possible solutions for a parking problem on a college campus. They were first asked to list all of the solutions they could think of on their own; then a panel of experts assessed the ideas to determine which were the best.

The interesting part came when they were asked afterwards how many of the good ideas they had come up with personally and how many had been generated by others in the group. Consistently, people overestimated how many of the 'good' ideas they had thought of on their own. On average, they each believed that they had come up with 75% of the best ideas, when in reality, they had come up with 30% of them. It turns out that we have a demonstrable tendency to overestimate our own capacity to solve problems in the absence of other input.

> We have a demonstrable tendency to overestimate our own capacity to solve problems in the absence of other input.

Maybe that's not too surprising. By definition, we each see the world from our own perspective, so what seems 'right' to us is what has been confirmed by our own experience. We all think we have a pretty good handle on how the world works, so it seems somewhat natural that we tend to undervalue others' perspectives when they differ from our own—or even simply bring experience that we have not had. While it may be natural to stick with our own ideas, though, it is demonstrably less effective in addressing problems and working for positive change.

Who Is At The Table?

Another significant value of working in community is that if we are truly engaged with our communities, then more stakeholders are represented in the conversation. If we want to work on issues of homelessness and don't welcome the people most directly affected—

people who are experiencing homelessness—into the conversation regarding what is needed and how we can work together to meet those needs, then we are unlikely to meet them. That seems like an obvious error, but it is certainly not an uncommon one. If we have those conversations among people who are experiencing homelessness and people who are concerned about their needs, but law enforcement, social workers, local businesses, people already working on the issue, etc., are not in the conversation, too, then we are also unlikely to come up with the best strategies to meet everyone's needs, and the solutions we propose are unlikely to be sustainable.

This is particularly true among groups that locate themselves more in the mainstream than in the margins. It is fundamental to the nature of privilege that it is extremely hard for the privileged to perceive; it has to be taught from the margins. This means that White people, men, straight people, people with no obvious physical or mental disabilities, wealthy people, etc. must be extremely intentional about listening and learning. That is important as a means, but also in order to achieve effective ends. Power tends to be concentrated among people who are privileged, and among people who are accustomed to having such power. It just seems 'normal'. If many of the voices in a community are not being heard, however, then the conclusions reached by the powerful will not be tenable. There is significant perspective and insight lacking, and the interests of all stakeholders are not being taken into account.

Once again, this work of community involves a heavy dose of listening. Listening skills, though manifestly teachable, are seldom taught, and that is to our detriment. Rather than telling each other what we think and asking others what they think, we too often tell our opponents what *they* think. "Sure, but when you people say..., what you mean is...!" So we end up arguing with imaginary adversaries rather than hearing the concerns of real people, which tend to be a bit more nuanced than we imagine. That approach has not served us well, and it doesn't show much sign of serving us better in the future.

I've been taking this to heart lately in my own work and

experimenting with bringing more voices into my own decision-making, both in the creative areas of my life and in the business aspects. It has proven to have all the value that I had hoped. I have enjoyed a rich relationship with the editor I hired for this book and some insightful first readers who have offered useful feedback, bringing some other perspective that I don't have. I have enjoyed some great artistic collaborations on some songwriting I've done in recent years, as well. But the deepest ongoing impact that this new, community-centered approach has had for me might be the change I've made in the way I handle event bookings.

Rather than telling each other what we think and asking others what they think, we too often tell our opponents what they think.

I have a tendency to say yes to too many invitations to speak and perform, and this has a very real cost for me, for my family, and eventually, for the quality of my work. In an effort to do a better job with discernment, and on the advice of some wise mentors, I have begun a new process in my own scheduling. I used to decide which engagement invitations I would accept more or less on my own, in consultation with my booking agent. Now, all booking decisions run through a booking committee which meets at my house twice a month.

That committee consists of my booking agent, my manager, my wife, and myself. We look at each invitation in the context of other calendar commitments around it as well as the various things I value in an invitation, which include not only the fee, but also the opportunity for impact, the chance that an event will lead to other good events, personal relationships, support for a cause I believe in, and many other factors. We do a much better job together of considering those categories and their relative weight than I do by myself. As a result, I'm saner, less exhausted, and doing better work.

It's also right that more stakeholders be represented. My calendar of commitments has significant impact on everyone at the meeting, especially my wife, Deanna. If she is involved in those decisions on the front end of the process, then we can make those choices together. Deanna has always been extraordinarily supportive of my work, in spite of the fact that my frequent absences have real costs for her. With this new process, though, I think we are diminishing the possibility of understandable resentments. We are making these decisions together.

Another advantage of working in community is that over time it brings an inherent accountability. By working together, we come to know and understand each others' strengths and weaknesses, our character and style, and that elevates the quality of our work and also of our daily lives. People who show themselves to be dependable and invested tend to be highly valued in a community. People who are difficult and destructive are not. In my small town, for example, I have noticed that businesses that are run by disagreeable people tend not to last too long. Accountability is a part of the inherent beauty of community.

Not Alone

The last lens I want to hold up and use to examine community is *solidarity*. The term has become politically loaded, but it should not be dismissed by anyone who wants to have a positive impact, regardless of where on the political spectrum they sit. It's a term with evolving meanings, and I believe that I understand it now much better than I did only a few years ago, having spent my first night in jail in the interim.

I was arrested, along with six other men, in May of 2011 for disrupting the North Carolina Legislature from the balcony while the legislators below deliberated the largest cut to public education funding in the history of the state, changes to voter laws that would have the effect of suppressing minority votes, and the gutting of the North Carolina Racial Justice Act. This groundbreaking law allowed death penalty defendants to present evidence of racism in their cases as part of their defense and appeals process. If their claims were determined to have merit, their sentences could be reduced from death to life in prison. It did not set anyone free; it just allowed for appeals based on evidence of racism and prevented the state from killing someone if they won that appeal.

The law had passed only two years before, and it was already under attack. The group I was with was focusing on several issues, and I felt strongly about each of them, but it was the Racial Justice Act that somehow went right to my core and convinced me to join them in a protest which might result in spending time in jail. Rev. Dr. William Barber, the head of the North Carolina NAACP, was and still is the leader of the effort to challenge the goals of the current legislative majority. This action was an early iteration of what later turned into the Forward Together movement that has gained national and even international attention in the years since, due to their large and sustained Moral Mondays protests.

That day, Rev. Barber, myself, and many others stood in the balcony overlooking the North Carolina House of Representatives while they were in session. Rev. Barber asked the Speaker of the House the same question that the prophet Micah had asked in the Bible, "What does the Lord require of you?" Rev. Curtis Gatewood, another NAACP leader, and others around him began chanting Micah's response to his own question, "Do justice. Love mercy. Walk humbly with God," which, it turns out, works pretty well as a chant.

Several people in the group were removed from the chamber, handcuffed, and taken in the backs of police cruisers to the jail, where we were charged with second degree trespassing and disorderly conduct. We were photographed, processed, fingerprinted, and taken to a holding cell, where we spent a few hours, with other prisoners occasionally coming and going. Each hour, on the hour, we took turns leading a prayer. We talked with the other people there about their situations. We sang, we told stories, and we talked strategy, deciding together that we would not post bail yet, though it was available to us. Part of the fundamental basis of nonviolent resistance is that it is intended to expose systemic injustice. If good, principled people are in jail, the reasoning goes, then perhaps there is some lack of goodness and principle in the system that is putting them there. We wanted to shine a little more light on the immorality of what was happening in the legislature, so we decided not to leave jail quite yet. Four of the group were pastors, and it's probably fair to say that all of us were generally well-respected.

While getting arrested for the first time was personally significant for me, I was quickly reminded of how small my place in the struggle for justice really was as I listened to dramatic stories told by Rev. Barber and Rev. Kojo Nantambu, who was around when the Wilmington Ten were arrested. As we sat together in the holding cell, Rev. Nantambu talked about the siege of the church where the African American community had gathered for refuge, how a man with whom he was standing arm-in-arm was shot and fell to the ground right beside him. Though these stories were hard to hear, they certainly put our current action into perspective, and it was a gift to me to hear them in that particular time and place. They shrank our own situation and sacrifice down to size.

> I don't intend to argue in this book that more dramatic and seemingly larger efforts and sacrifices are not sometimes necessary, or that they are not sometimes yours to do. What I do argue is that they are not the sensible starting place.

Nevertheless, I was scared. I didn't know what was going to happen, and I had little to no control over the situation. Even as I understood that this action was quite small in the history of the struggle for civil rights, it was a pretty big deal for me personally.

When we were admitted, we were taken out of the room one at a time. I was stripped of my clothing, the contents of my pockets and my wedding ring (one of the few times it has left my finger since I first put it on), and strip-searched, standing naked before a guard who made me spread my feet apart and adjust my body so that he had a good view. I was given orange-striped jail clothes, several sizes too large.

After we had each been through that same routine and waited a while longer, we were manacled by one wrist to a chain connecting eight prisoners and led through an elevator to the general holding cells. It had been several hours by this time, but the lights were still on and the prisoners still sitting at tables playing games or standing around in the common area when we arrived. We were each told to grab a thin, plastic-covered mattress from a stack outside the door and then go inside.

Tuning our own notes together so that we are in harmony, while each having different voices, is extremely difficult.

Just inside the door, facing us, was a muscular man with dreadlocks and tattoos covering his neck and all the visible parts of his arms and chest. He grinned and said, "Welcome to Cell Block Green, gentlemen." Though I tried to figure it out, I had no idea whether that smile was friendly or not. I decided to assume that it was. The remote-control steel and glass door moved into place behind us, the sound of its whirring motor ending in a metallic locking sound.

The jail was overcrowded and the cells were all full, so some of us slept (or rather, laid down) on the floor in the common area along with roughly two-dozen other prisoners. That felt vulnerable, and well out of my experience, so sleep was out of the question for me.

I cannot imagine going through the arrest and night in jail without those other men with me. The powerful solidarity of that experience will stay with me forever. Rev. Nantambu smiling and leading the manacled prisoner train in a tight u-turn in the jail's elevator (no buttons on the inside, just a camera) so we would be pointing the right way when the door opened again. Rev. Barber

Rev. Kojo Nantambu, Rev. Curtis Gatewood and me

leading songs, educating us and keeping spirits up. The dignity and grace of Rev. Spearman and the others. Some joking and some processing of what was going on. That's how we get through the hardest days and the hardest work we have to do. As my friend Chuck Brodsky sings, "We keep each other going and we show each other signs." It's the deepest gift of such a struggle—knowing in your bones that you are not alone.

It may seem contradictory to include this story about spending a night in jail when I've just spent so many pages arguing for the importance and effectiveness of small efforts. Depending on your life experience, jail may or may not seem like a very big deal, but it likely sounds rather drastic when compared to some of the efforts I've described so far—making copies, for example. Regardless, I don't think it undermines the argument for small efforts.

I don't intend to argue in this book that more dramatic and

seemingly larger efforts and sacrifices are not sometimes necessary, or that they are not sometimes yours to do. What I do argue is that they are not the sensible starting place. It is not wise to walk into the gym and try to pick up the heaviest weights you see. You have to work out, and it helps to learn good technique. For that, you need mentors and teachers, which may be most easily found in community. The first step, though, and arguably the hardest one, is actually showing up at the gym.

Community is a powerful force for change. In our adventure at the State House, no one of us alone would have caused the media attention or community discussion that we all did together: five Black, two White; four ministers, one musician. We generated a fair amount of conversation, and though the gutting of the North Carolina Racial Justice Act passed, it was vetoed by the governor and narrowly missed having enough votes for an override. I'd like to think we had something to do with one or both of those last points, just by getting people talking about the issue, perhaps serving as the catalyst for some of them to contact their representatives and get more involved.

The blog I wrote about our arrest on the North Carolina Council of Churches web site still holds the record for the most views on that site. In the weeks that followed our arrests, I saw comment after comment on Facebook and in other places saying, "I had no idea that this was happening!" Most of us are understandably busy with our lives and other obligations, and it is no wonder that we fail to keep up with everything happening in our state capitols. It is our duty to keep up with it, but it not surprising that we often miss the mark. Those comments were what I wanted to see—people who didn't know before but did now.

In community, in the context of real and interwoven relationships, we can support, nourish, educate, and challenge each other in ways that are constructive rather than destructive. We can devise more effective and wiser strategies than we can create on our own. We can hold each other accountable and catch each other when we stumble. We can move forward together, deep in the knowledge that we are not alone.

I shouldn't move on without saying one more important thing about community: it's hard. Tuning our own notes together so that we are in harmony, while each having different voices, is extremely difficult. Welcoming diversity of opinion and listening closely and compassionately while disagreeing is hard. Finding ways to work with people we find challenging is hard. Discerning where the lines are regarding when someone can no longer be welcomed into the community is hard. Showing up in situations where you have traditionally been disregarded is hard. Setting aside privilege and yielding power is hard.

According to my aforementioned buddy Hugh, the only thing harder is the lack of community.

CHAPTER TEN

Creativity & Worldchanging

*If you have built castles in the air, your work
need not be lost; that is where they should be.
Now put the foundations under them.*

— Henry David Thoreau

On May 26, 2007, the Ku Klux Klan and neo-Nazi groups gathered for a rally in Knoxville, Tennessee. The defendants in a local murder case were African American, and some White supremacists from out of town drove there to protest. The general tone of their rally was unsurprisingly hateful. One man in camouflage held up a hand-drawn poster with a picture of a noose and the words "insert neck here" scrawled beside it, expressing his preference for a lynching over a trial.

Most people in Knoxville were not pleased to have the Klan come to town, but how should they respond? The first two natural responses to aggression, built into our psyches at a very deep level, are quite familiar in this kind of situation: fight and flight. On the one hand, we are tempted to go down to the rally and give them a piece of our minds. "We'll see how tough they are when we have a bigger crowd and we shout louder!"

On the other, people will often say, "Ignore them. They just want attention," which is more or less a form of retreat.

The problem with the first approach is that, in the words of Dr. King, it adds "deeper darkness to a night already devoid of stars." Meeting hatred with hatred only increases the amount of hatred in the world. That may sound idealistic, but I am convinced that it is the heart of pragmatism. In this particular case, the Klan *does* thrive on anger and opposition. They love it, and adding our hatred to theirs is no more effective in opposing their message than trying to put out a grass fire by dousing it with gasoline.

The problem with the second approach, in its most usual form of 'just staying home', is that it allows damaging and hateful rhetoric to be broadcast unopposed.[21] Such rallies will nearly always gather some kind of a crowd and media exposure, unless there is an organized effort to deny them one. When such hatred goes unopposed, the people who are being attacked by their rhetoric end up feeling abandoned by potential allies who could be standing with them.

They feel that way because they *are* being abandoned. "We will have to repent in this generation not merely for the hateful words and actions of the bad people but for the appalling silence of the good people," Martin Luther King, Jr. wrote in his famous "Letter From a Birmingham Jail."

So neither option is satisfactory, but what other options are there? That's a question that activists in Knoxville, led by members of an environmental activist group called Mountain Justice, asked themselves. By not assuming that the question was rhetorical, they came up with a wonderful and effective answer.

That day the Ku Klux Klan was met by the Coup Clutz Clowns, who had prepared carefully and found what theologian Walter Wink called a 'Third Way': neither fight nor flight, but a

---

21 It should be noted that 'just staying home' is different from organizing a freeze out. The former is generally an excuse for apathy. The latter is sometimes an effective strategy. The town of Davidson, North Carolina, organized an impressive example of this in 1986. When the KKK announced plans for a rally, students organized an activity day on the other side of town. They connected with local business owners and arranged for everything on the town square to be closed and for there to be no one there except for the Klansmen (they hid video cameras to document it). The Klansmen marched halfway down the street, then gave up and went home, since no one was watching. (http://www.davidsonian.com/news/common-ground-prepares-for-multi-cultural-event-1.2701125#.U1xiCMeaH4I)

I spoke at a similar event in 2013, 'The People's Conference on Race & Equality', organized by a coalition of activists in Memphis, Tennessee, which happened at the same time as a Klan rally downtown. (http://davidlamotte.com/2013/04/the-klan-went-home-the-community-stayed/)

The Coup Clutz Clowns in Knoxville (photo by Conrad Charleston)

creative way to transform violence and hatred—in this case with humor.

When the Klan began to chant, "White power!", the clowns pretended they couldn't quite understand what they were saying. They facetiously decided it must be a rally for "'White flour" and pulled out bags of flour they had brought with them. A big flour fight and much hilarity ensued.

After a while, the clowns decided they must have heard wrong, though, so they listened again and determined that these strange demonstrators were actually chanting "White flowers", which they then distributed to the crowd, laughing and clowning around as they did so.

When they had exhausted that gag, one clown pulled out a camp shower and the others tried to crowd beneath it, chanting, "Tight showers!" At some point, they started tossing toilet paper and chanting, "Wipe power!" Finally, they pulled on wedding dresses and crescendoed with, "Wife power!"

The Klan was baffled. They are accustomed to being feared and shouted at, but there was no response in their repertoire to a crowd across the street actually having a wonderful time. They left an hour and a half early, with only one arrest: a neo-Nazi who charged across the street toward the clowns.

As my friend Scott Shepherd, a former Klan leader who is now an anti-racism activist, wrote to me, "The Klan is successful with their public demonstrations only when they get the attention, feed off the hatred, and stir up negative emotions with the crowd. When the counter-protestors step up and take the control and attention away from the Klan, they fail with their attempt to get their negative message out. I have always heard that humor is the best medicine, and I believe this after witnessing the clowns' effect on the KKK demonstrations."

There is an invitation to transformation, not just a squashing of the opposition.

It is important to note here that none of these chants made fun of the Klan themselves. The clowns simply refused to take the Klan's ridiculous ideas seriously. So there is a window, however small, for the Klansmen to laugh too. There is an invitation to transformation, not just a squashing of the opposition.

They had found a Third Way—creative, non-violent engagement. It was hardly an obvious response, but when they invested creative energy in the question of how to respond, they came up with an option that was better than the ones to which we usually turn.

As John Lewis wrote in his book *Across That Bridge*, "Nonviolence is confrontational. It is not silent in the face of injustice, but 'creatively maladjusted.'" Nonviolence is not about passivity; it is fundamentally creative.

Artist Peter von Tiesenhausen was being threatened by oil corporations that wanted access to the natural gas beneath his 800 acre property in Alberta, Canada. Legally, the companies can lay claim to the land beneath private property, beneath a depth of six inches, but von Tiesenhausen didn't want his family farm, inherited from his parents, to be disturbed.

His solution? He created art across his land and copyrighted the entire thing, to a depth of six inches, which made any disturbance of the land a copyright violation. He also began to charge any oil industry companies that wanted to talk with him about his land a consultant's fee. "I demand $500 an hour. They pay. It keeps the meetings really short, and they don't do it nearly as often as they used to," the artist said.

Creativity is expressed through an act of creation. When we speak of creation, however, we tend to speak in scientific or religious terms (or an integration of the two). In both cases, we are generally referring to something that happened a long time ago and then was over.

It is important, and sometimes difficult, to remember that in relation to a given problem, the possibilities are not limited to the possibilities we can see.

That's not how it works.

The world is still being created. There is a blade of grass outside the cabin where I'm now writing in the southern foothills of Virginia that wasn't there a few weeks ago. Now it is. There is a flame in the fireplace that didn't exist two hours ago, before I built the fire.

And more importantly to me, there is a relationship being formed between you and me as you read these words. Depending on how long and how well we've known each other, that may be a new relationship just being created or an old one that is shifting somewhat because of this interaction, but regardless, there was a time before it existed and a time when it was new under the sun.

Julia Cameron, in her classic book on creativity, *The Artist's Way*, writes that "Creativity is the natural order of life." Life goes on, so creativity and creation do too.

Ongoing creation is an everyday miracle that we tend to disregard, or at least I do. I should be clear, though, that when I say 'miracle', I don't mean a case where the rules of science are apparently suspended and something entirely extraordinary happens. I mean that if we look at it closely, the existence and functionality of anything at all is beyond human comprehension. You, me, the laptop on my lap, the book you're reading—the atoms that make up all of them are made up of almost entirely empty space. Yet you exist. I exist. We both think and feel and grow and hurt and heal. The words that appear on my laptop screen as I type today will soon be printed on paper in a building I've never seen, and eventually, they'll find their way to you. Tell me there are no miracles, and I will simply hold up a mirror. *Everything* is a miracle.

It is important, and sometimes difficult, to remember that in relation to a given problem, the possibilities are not limited to the possibilities we can see. When logic dictates that we have exhausted all possible options, it helps to remember that miracles are commonplace. The world is constantly surprising us, and not all of the surprises are negative. If you hold out hope and work toward a good outcome to a bad situation, especially without a clear explanation of the path from here to there, you are likely to be dismissed as an idealist. History, however, does not stand entirely against you.

In the summer of 2008, I was part of an Interfaith Peace Delegation to Palestine and Israel with a group called Interfaith Peace-Builders. We visited people and places along the spectra of political, religious, and cultural context, having earnest and intense conversation with people of wildly varying convictions. It gave us a much broader view of the histories, cultures, and conflicts that pervade the region than we would have had if we had only visited holy sites or only talked with people on one of the many sides of that complicated conflict. We met with ideological Jewish settlers, Israeli and Palestinian students of various opinions and social strata, secular activists, and religious activists of various faiths. Each brought their own views and experience to an extremely complex situation, and helped us to understand their own suffering and that of people they love.[22]

Among the people we met with was a Palestinian activist in Ramallah named Omar Barghouti. He and an older activist spent some time with us, updating us on their efforts to put economic pressure on the state of Israel regarding their policies toward Palestine and Palestinians. In 2008, this was a fairly fresh push in that particular struggle, and Omar was one of the early leaders in that nonviolent effort. He shared a lot of interesting, and often discouraging, information with us.

The thing I remember most clearly, though, was at the end of our time together, sitting around a table at the Quaker Center in Ramallah. As is usually the case, what sticks with me is not data, but a personal story. Someone asked Omar how he maintains hope in the face of such a long struggle with ongoing injustice and so little sign of progress. How did he maintain the energy to keep up his work?

Tell me there are no miracles, and I will simply hold up a mirror. Everything is a miracle.

Omar is four years older than I am, so he was in college during some of the later years of the Apartheid regime in South Africa. He explained that during his college years, he was involved with the anti-Apartheid movement. In those days, South Africa's oppressive government had the support of the world's powers. The United States and other countries had significant financial investments in the Apartheid regime, and it seemed to be in their best interests to defend the status quo. It was a struggle of the powerless against the powerful, and the only real thing the former had on their side was that they were right; the system they were struggling against was unjust. There was no rational justification for optimism.

Yet the miracle came. After 27 years of incarceration, Nelson

---

22 I highly recommend the trip and the organization. They take delegations each year, and you can reach them at www.ifpb.org.

Mandela was released from prison. Four years later he was elected president. The bloodbath of retributive ethnic cleansing that most people predicted when 'the Blacks' came to power never occurred. As history would have it, the idealists turned out to be the realists in this situation.

Back in Ramallah, Mr. Barghouti explained, "We see what happened in South Africa. No one can tell me that nothing can change here in Palestine. No one can tell me now that I am foolish to hope."

As history would have it, the idealists turned out to be the realists in this situation.

And what of the fall of the Berlin wall? Those who predicted German reunification would also have been laughed out of the room—until it happened. We should not allow ourselves to be immobilized by the apparent bleakness of circumstances. History has a way of surprising us.

Rosa Parks, at the end of her autobiography, published in 1992, wrote with wonder, "Thirty years ago no one would have believed that Jesse Jackson, a Black man, could run for president of the United States and get White votes in the state primary elections."

If only she had lived a few years longer. Rosa Parks herself, given her own experience of racism and oppression, might have laughed at you if you had suggested that the United States would elect a Black president within four years of her death. Or maybe not. She certainly had no shortage of vision and hope, and she had seen and contributed to remarkable changes in her own lifetime.

We have come to a time in history when we have a tendency to equate cynicism with realism and hope with naiveté, but that is simply not accurate.

College students, youth at camp retreats, people at music festivals, and others having 'mountaintop' experiences commonly refer to returning to the 'real world', as though these short-term gatherings aren't also part of the real world. They are no less real than anywhere else, and if they are especially nourishing and life-giving for us, we shouldn't dismiss them as 'unreal'; we should try to figure out how we can make the rest of the world a bit more like them.

Twice a year, thousands of people gather on a hot, dusty ranch in Kerrville, Texas, for the Kerrville Folk Festival. For eighteen days each spring and a few more in the fall, music flows through sound systems on big stages and through acoustic instruments in the campgrounds. Longtime friends gather in makeshift neighborhoods where they have gathered for years and catch up on the year's news and a new crop of songs. It is a kind place, where eccentricities are at least tolerated, often celebrated, and where attendees catch a glimpse of what a kinder and more tolerant world might look like. Near the front gate there is a sign. that says, "Welcome home." Nearby, there is another sign that says, "It can be this way always."

This could easily (and reasonably) be dismissed as foolish idealism, or it could be embraced as a vision to work toward. The first step in changing the 'real world' is to imagine a better way, but we have a tendency to shut down the voices of those who articulate such ideas. "You may say I'm a dreamer," John Lennon wrote, quite familiar with the charge of being an idealist.

But perhaps an 'ideal-ist' is better defined as one who can envision ideals. That doesn't necessarily mean one who confuses reality with an imagined perfect circumstance. It can also mean one who is committed to moving

photo by Neale Eckstein

closer to that better scenario. If we cannot envision a better way, we have little hope of creating it. The first step is the creative phase—the imagining; the second is building the bridge from here to there.

Poets have been trying to get this point across for some time. Thoreau describes these two steps to creation, "If you have built castles in the air, your work need not be lost; that is where they should be. Now put the foundations under them." Emily Dickinson said it another way, "The possible's slow fuse is lit by the imagination."

We have come to a time in history when we have a tendency to equate cynicism with realism and hope with naiveté, but that is simply not accurate.

Creativity is necessary in the pursuit of worldchanging. As my friend Dan Nichols sings, "If you do what you've always done, you'll get what you've always gotten, you'll be who you've always been, you'll go where you've always gone."[23] Worldchanging is not a multiple choice activity. It involves creating more options than you're initially presented with.

Generally, though, we look at a big problem, can't see a solution, and throw up our hands. If no one has figured it out yet, we reason that we are unlikely to do so. But the truth is that people are discovering and developing new ways to approach problems every day. It might make more sense to look at a problem, gather people together, and make space for ideas to unfold. In order to be creative, we have to be intentional and invite that creativity.

The respected conflict transformation theorist and practitioner John Paul Lederach discussed his experience of creative and artistic moments in peace-building work:

---

[23] This quotation shows up in various forms, in various places, with quite a few different attributions. Dan has spent considerable energy trying to find the original source with no luck, so I'm quoting Dan. dannicholsmusic.com

I have found that transformative moments in conflict are many times those filled with a haiku-like quality that floods a particular process or space. We might call them the moments of the aesthetic imagination, a place where suddenly, out of complexity and historic difficulty, the clarity of great insight makes an unexpected appearance in the form of an image or in a way of putting something that can only be described as artistic.

We are wise to explore cultivating artful and creative approaches to tasks that we generally consider to be rational, like negotiation and conflict transformation. But beyond that, we are also wise to consider including art by its more conventional definition in our work of worldchanging, weaving it into situations where we might not expect to encounter it.

Art, as we generally think of it, has huge potential to shift emotional context and change the tone of a conflict in ways that rational argument cannot. In recent years, well- respected peacemakers and academics like Lederach, Howard Zehr, my former professor Roland Bleiker, and many others have pointed to the significance of art in peace work.

They are not the first ones to make such observations. The famed Russian actor and theater director Konstantin Sergeievich Stanislavski, the father of 'method acting', argued in 1926 that the best actors could convey their meanings clearly, even across cultural and language barriers. "The theatre" he said, "is one of the best and principal means of bringing about reconciliation and mutual understanding between nations."

In 2006, 25 people, both Sunnis and Shias, gathered under a large tent in downtown Baghdad, Iraq, to share poetry. They had come at the invitation of Yanar Mohammed, a prominent Iraqi women's rights activist, who had a vision for peacemaking through poetry. Kim Rosen, the author of *Saved By a Poem: The Transformative Power of Words*, writes that, "The Shiites sit opposite the Sunnis, thinking it will be a competition. But by the end of the event, all are embracing and dancing together—because the poems from both sides voice the same words, the same longings, the same wounds." In subsequent years, the event grew dramatically, and, according to the organizer of the event, "with this ball of magic being bounced from one side to the other... they all turned out to be on the same team!"

This shift can also occur in contexts that are not rife with conflict. At the first National Conference on Restorative Justice, held in Texas in 2007, I was invited to introduce the plenary speakers. Along with the standard speaker introduction, noting their qualifications and the topics they would address, the people organizing the conference asked me to introduce each speaker with a topical song and story. It was a delightful challenge and a fascinating strategy. Before moving into the sometimes heady topics to be addressed by leading academics and practitioners from around the world, we had a chance as a group to open our hearts for a moment, to consider why this particular topic matters and feel that significance.

If we cannot envision a better way, we have little hope of creating it.

And it worked. Once again, what seemed to be the least 'serious' part of our work together shifted the mood in the room in ways that I believe mattered a great deal, putting us in the right frame of mind to engage deeply with the ideas being presented.

In another effort to approach a serious topic through art, I put the story of the clowns and the Klan to rhyme and began to perform the poem in my concerts. Then in 2012, I teamed up with illustrator Jenn Hales to publish a children's book about it.

The book has gone on to have some wonderful adventures and has received accolades from people like Dr. Patch Adams, the real-life clown activist who was the subject of the Robin Williams movie that bore his name, along with eminent nonviolence theorists Gene Sharp and Johann Galtung. It received favorable coverage from the Southern Poverty Law Center and several other organizations I admire, and I have a picture of John Lewis holding the book and smiling. It was even recently set to music and recorded by folksinger Rod MacDonald. It has had quite a life. The original clown action was wonderfully creative, and I can't help but believe that the story has traveled even farther due to its re-telling in rhyme, visual art, and song.

As thrilled as I was by all of that, though, by far the most wonderful part of the book's story happened six months after it came out. In November of 2012, there was a neo-Nazi rally in Charlotte, North Carolina, a couple of hours from my own home. The counter-protestors, led by Charlotte's Latino Coalition, dressed as clowns, brought bags of flour to the rally, and took their scripting directly from the poem. NBC News ran national stories on it, including an interview with a City Councilman wearing a red foam nose.

The next morning, my email inbox blew up with people asking if I had been involved, but I had nothing to do with it other than writing the poem. I later contacted the lead organizer, and she confirmed that they had heard my poem and been inspired by the Knoxville clowns, just as I was.

It matters which stories we tell. If our actions are guided by our stories, then it is worthwhile to create and curate better visions within them. Creativity is essential to the work of positive change, and vision is the first step in that process.

CHAPTER ELEVEN

Stumbling Toward the Light

*We learn a lot from the mistakes of others,
but even more from our own.*

— Fausto Cercignani

I've been married twice. Conveniently for me, they were both to the same woman and only a few weeks apart. Deanna and I decided to have two ceremonies—what we refer to as our 'introvert wedding' and our 'extrovert wedding'. The former was a simple, quiet Quaker wedding with forty or so people, and the latter was a pot-luck, music-festival-style affair for 400 in the center of the Warren Wilson College campus, complete with frisbees, bands playing all day, and a clown parade populated by the children of our friends.

In the middle of the afternoon, we were ready to have the actual service under an open-air pavilion, but it was overcast and warm, and our friends were comfortable on their blankets in the grass and reluctant to come under the pavilion. Deanna and I waited at the campus gym to walk down together through the grass and into the pavilion, but we weren't quite sure what to do when friends declined to gather.

Then someone cued the rain. The clouds let down their precious cargo, and everyone dashed under the pavilion. A few minutes later it stopped, as suddenly as it had started. It was the only rain we had all day, and it couldn't have been scripted any better.

We had decided that we would go on our honeymoon between the two weddings, but we couldn't quite decide where to go. There is no shortage of beauty in the world, and this was, we hoped, a once-in-a-lifetime trip. Which tropical island? Which glorious mountain range?

We were still kicking those questions around when Deanna and I ran into her friend Stacey. Stacey had just returned from attending a language immersion school in Guatemala. She had stayed with a Guatemalan family and studied Spanish during the day at a school that she highly recommended. Her descriptions were enticing, and Deanna said, "We could do *that* for our honeymoon!" We chuckled. Then we looked at each other. "We could," I said.

And we did. We spent a couple of weeks in Antigua, Guatemala, a beautiful town largely populated with tourists. Still, even in Antigua, or 'Gringotenango' as it is sometimes called, we encountered plenty of people who speak no English and plenty of opportunities to build our budding language skills.

We thoroughly enjoyed our experience, studying five hours a day with our own private tutors for two and a half weeks. We lived with a Guatemalan family who spoke only Spanish. Kids, it turns out, are excellent language teachers. They have smaller vocabularies, so they naturally start with the basics. They also don't mind repeating things over and over until you get it.

We spent the weekends on the more traditional honeymoon fare of Mayan temple ruins and a side trip to the idyllic Lago Atítlan, but we spent most of our time studying, and thus earned our lifetime nerd credentials by actually going to school on our honeymoon.

The school we attended, Probigua, uses its profits to support libraries in rural villages. It also runs two mobile libraries built into school buses that circulate to areas that would otherwise have virtually no access to books. On Fridays, they invite their *extranjero* students to come along on trips to those villages to deliver supplies, and Deanna and I were both looking forward to that trip on our first Friday there.

As it turned out, though, I got some sort of intestinal bug that took me out of commission on the morning of the trip. I encouraged Deanna to go anyway, and she did, having a wonderful adventure in the mountains, complete with the school bus they were riding on sliding off the road into a mud bank, requiring all of its passengers to push to get it back in the track. They took some paint, books, and a couple of computers to a library that Probigua supported in the hills not far away.

Back at the school on Monday, I was chatting with my tutor (and now friend), Claritza Morales, about how sorry I was to miss that opportunity, and she offered a possible alternative. Looking across the class room, which is really more of a tin-roofed pavilion, she pointed out another of the teachers there. Claritza explained that the other teacher had a sister who taught in a public school in the mountains nearby, and that she could ask whether we could go for a visit.

I have never been as interested in tourist destinations as I am in cross-cultural experiences. The sites that we can all agree are amazing are less interesting to me than an opportunity to understand what normal, everyday life is like for people— and, in doing so, to shake myself out of my own assumptions. It is deceptively easy for me to assume that my lifestyle in the U.S. is a normal one and to forget that it is quite unusual on a world scale.

Statistically, I'm an aberration in many ways. Having multiple pairs of shoes, for instance, sets me apart from the majority of the world's population as fairly wealthy.

Because it was outside of my normal experience and provided a glimpse of someone else's daily life, visiting a public school in a small, non-tourist-infested village in Guatemala was extremely interesting to me.

Claritza spoke with her colleague, who got in touch with her sister, and a few days later we went into the mountains, up roads that were sometimes paved and sometimes mud, past burros and pigs and campesinos, until we found ourselves in the village of Santa Lucia Milpas Altas.

The director of the school met us at the chain link fence that surrounded the school and welcomed us. He was young, bespectacled, and professional. It was easy to see he was proud of the school, though his eyebrows drew together when he spoke of struggles they were facing, overcrowding prominent among them. A bit down the road from the school, only accessible via a small dirt path, there was a cinderblock building they were using for some classes. It seemed to be a house that was half-finished, with several rooms inside but no windows. A single lightbulb hung from the center of the bare room, with worn student chairs packed against each other along the walls. Someone had made an effort to brighten the space with some colorful cutouts of Disney characters and the word 'Bienvenidos' in orange paper letters taped to one wall, but the tape wasn't holding on the rough cinderblock, so the last few letters of the word lay folded over and hanging down the wall.

The rest of the school was mostly in better shape than that, and, in fact, better than I would find at many other schools I would visit in coming years. Still, they were facing real challenges. As the principal continued to show me around, several of them became particularly evident.

The school had 218 students. In addition to not having room for all of them, one of the major problems was the condition of the bathrooms. That was part of my tour, too. They had North American-style facilities, but they were in extremely bad shape, with some of the sinks on the floor and some of the toilets broken. That wasn't the primary problem, though. The real issue was that they had no running water.

Somehow the bathrooms had been built without tying them into the well, which was about twenty feet away (and yes, uphill, by the slope of the land). The principal explained that he wanted very much to run plumbing and a pump from the well to the bathrooms, but that it simply wasn't in the school's budget. I asked if he knew how much it would cost, and he said yes, that it would be about a thousand *quetzales*. I did the math in my head, which is *never* a good idea in my case. Sure enough, I thought, I must have done it wrong; one thousand *quetzales* appeared to be about 125 U.S. dollars.

Having spent plenty of time, like many of us have, reading the news and feeling powerless to have any kind of positive impact on problems so large, I suddenly felt incredibly empowered. At that point Deanna was working as a public school teacher, and I was a folksinger. We weren't considered affluent by any means in our own cultural context—but $125? We could do that.

But how is it that there wasn't budget for $125 to run plumbing to the bathrooms?

That was the day that I began to learn about the lack of funding for public schools in Guatemala. Government funding of education has actually improved significantly in the decade since I visited that school, though a massive shortfall remains.

At that point, though, the Guatemalan government generally only paid for public school teachers' salaries, and nothing else. Not the building, not the electricity, not the textbooks—which is why many Guatemalan schools don't *have* textbooks. The schools have to raise the money for the bare essentials from the parents of the students, many of whom are living in abject poverty.

In recent years, the government has passed laws requiring that public education be entirely free, but the increases in funding do not appear to be commensurate. This has had the effect of increasing the rolls at schools, but decreasing the material support per student.

Of course, the needs of the school didn't stop with the plumbing. As we walked around a bit more, the director pointed out the two women who were crouched down by a well that dropped straight down in the middle of the school's cement courtyard, covered by a flat steel door. They were hauling water up and shucking corn to make food for the kids.

It turned out that this particular school had a much-coveted extra grant from the government to feed the children, the equivalent of ten cents per child per day. Feeding children at school is especially important because it provides an incentive for parents to actually send their kids. Many children in Guatemala do not go to school; their parents did not go to school, and they are needed at home to help with the manual labor of subsistence agriculture, weaving, or whatever the family's work may be.

The women were preparing beans, tortillas, and *atol de elote* (a traditional Mayan drink made from sweet corn, corn starch, water, and sugar) for the children, using a small butane stove. They were working in a space the size of an oversized closet, with dirty walls and paint over the window panes. It was clear that the school very much needed a kitchen as well. $850 would be enough for them to have one. So a thousand dollars would take care of both projects, with $25 to spare.

Standing there at the school that day, I had spent enough time in developing countries to understand that showing up and passing out money can be much more destructive than constructive. I didn't pull out my checkbook, and I didn't promise to send money, but I did commiserate with the director in his frustration, and I did ask for his contact information before I left.

As much as my heart had leapt at the thought that I could simply take care of the plumbing issue, $1,000 is a bit different than $125 for this folksinger. I could have written that check, and it wouldn't have bounced, but some other checks might have, as a result, when we got home.

Still, I felt the tug to engage, and I was eager to talk with Deanna about what we could afford and how to best begin building that relationship with the school that would allow us to do this together, with some mutuality and trust established. I didn't want to be paternalistic or propagate rich North American/poor Latin American stereotypes. And yet here was a very real need for some very real children. We were being asked to help, and it seemed that we had the means to address it.

These were not indolent, charity-seeking slackers, as people who are poor are so often portrayed. They were ordinary people working hard to provide an education for children in their community with meager resources, and it seemed that a small boost could make a significant difference. Certainly the hygiene of the students would improve with improvements to the bathrooms and the kitchen. That could have a significant effect on their health and therefore their school attendance.

And then I remembered what I do for a living: travel around, sing songs for people, and tell them stories. What if I told people the story of this school and asked if they would like to help out? We could use our own money to cover the costs of getting back down here and arranging the details so that anyone who wanted to chip in could know that 100% of their donation was going to the project. That way I could spend my few hundred dollars on the plane ticket and incidentals and still have $1,000 for the school. I could leverage our donation into more resources for the school than we could afford to donate ourselves.

Here was a very real need for some very real children. We were being asked to help, and it seemed that we had the means to address it.

So I did. When we returned home, I told the audiences at my next few concerts about this school and its needs, and I explained that if folks wanted to chip in, I would take the money back and see the project through. At my first three concerts, people chipped in the money we needed. As I recall, there was one $200 check in the basket we put out at the CD table, but most of the donations were in small denominations. People would buy a $15 CD after the concert and donate the $5 change to the Guatemalan effort, or even just throw in the coins in their pockets.

It had been so effortless to raise that money, and we could already see how far it could go in Guatemala. So we began to dream a little. What if we kept going? There was certainly no end of need in Guatemalan schools. Why not keep it up and address some needs in other schools?

So I checked my touring schedule and booked another ticket to Guatemala for the first gap I saw, in November. As it turned out, the contact information I had for the principal wasn't getting me in touch with him. The phone number seemed to be wrong or outdated, and he had not given me an email address. I knew I could contact him through Claritza and her co-worker when I got back to Guatemala, so I just booked the trip.

I built in a bit of time to visit some other people we had met on the trip and contacted Dennis Smith, a mission co-worker for the Presbyterian Church (U.S.A.), then based in Guatemala City. Another mission co-worker, Karla Koll, had been living and working in Guatemala for years and knew my sister from seminary, so I got in touch with her as well on a subsequent trip. I also dropped a note to David Glanville, a salty and colorful ex-pat hotel owner I had met at Lago Atítlan. We had stayed at his beautiful posada on the lake on one of our two honeymoon weekends between classes. I told these new friends that I was interested in learning more about local schools and that I had a plan to provide some small grants. Each of them was appropriately cautionary and encouraging at the same time. All three would help to nuance my understanding, introduce me to other good connections, and mentor me through the years since, though I'll admit I didn't ask them quite enough questions at the outset.

> It had been so effortless to raise that money, and we could already see how far it could go in Guatemala. So we began to dream a little.

When I got back to Guatemala a few months later, I realized I had made a big and novice mistake. It was November, and Guatemalan schools don't run on a North American schedule. They run from January to October. No one was to be found at the school in Santa Lucia Milpas Altas. I felt pretty stupid, and my efforts to track the principal down were fruitless. He was out of town.

I was back in Guatemala, though, and had started to investigate these new possibilities, so I followed up with the other folks I wanted to catch up with. One of the men who works at David Glanville's posada in Santiago is an engaging Mayan man named Nino Tecún. When I made my way back to Santiago, Nino took me to his nearby village, Tzanchaj, to show me a small preschool he ran for fourteen children in a rented room. The preschool-sized desks were crammed into the tiny space, and Nino explained that there were many more children in the village that would like to attend, but there was only room for fourteen. Nino himself had only finished third grade, but he has an entrepreneurial spirit, and he wanted his own children and the others in the village to have a fair shot at school. He had collected and contributed the money to pay a teacher to come teach the children and had opened the tiny school on his own, without any government or international support.

Before I first visited Guatemala, I naively thought it was a Spanish-speaking country, but many people in Guatemala, especially rural people and women, do not speak Spanish at all. Even for many of the people who do speak Spanish, it is often a second language; Mayan languages are most people's native tongues. At that time, however, public schools often only taught in Spanish, so the Mayan children were at a strong disadvantage if they didn't go to preschool and get a start on Spanish. More recently, laws requiring bilingual education have been passed, but in many places, Mayan-language education remains poor in quality.

On that trip, I started meeting with Nino and learning more about his school and how it might move forward to better serve his community. A year later, we had built a sturdy one-room school house for $2,500, complete with electricity. Today, due to contributions from other donors as well as our own continued involvement, it has three rooms, sixty-one students, indoor plumbing, a simple kitchen, and two teachers. They surprised me by naming it *Escuelita David LaMotte*, which is simultaneously moving and awkward.

In addition to Nino's school, PEG has now worked with over a dozen other schools and libraries in Guatemala, serving different needs in each community, based on the needs and desires of the local population, and partnering with other organizations that have deep relationships in places where we don't.

But what about the original school that inspired the project? My concert schedule was demanding, and it was going to be some time before I could come back to Guatemala, so my next idea was to ask Claritza, my friend and erstwhile Spanish teacher, to go and visit the principal to discuss options. When she went, I learned something else about Guatemala that I had not understood previously. Culturally, a female teacher has a hard time negotiating with the male principal of a school. As Claritza reported it to me, the principal was happy to hear of the interest, but he wanted to add some things in to the project. The inherent power imbalance made the conversation more of a negotiation than a dialogue, so Claritza made no promises and went home.

In the meantime, more projects were emerging, and they were going beautifully. I brought home pictures of the progress we were making with Nino's school and others, and people were only too happy to contribute. Many people have a natural and healthy skepticism of large non-profits, having seen the substantial overhead that some of them support and how little of their donations actually make it all the way to the projects. Because Deanna and I were absorbing all of the overhead, though (and keeping it to a minimum), and because my listeners feel like they know and trust me, they were only too eager to contribute.

We decided to pursue 501c3 non-profit status and put together a little organization. We chose the name PEG Partners. P.E.G. stands for Proyecto para las Escuelas Guatemaltecas, or Guatemalan School Project. A 'peg' is also the part of a guitar that tunes a string, so that made some sense for me, sitting at the intersection of music and education. Tiny changes in the orientation of a tuning peg on a guitar can make a huge difference to the quality of a song, and the same idea holds true for our work in Guatemala. Small efforts have proven to have substantial effect.

It was several more months before I could get back to Guatemala again, but when I did, I made another effort to visit the school in Santa Lucia, only to miss the principal yet again. He had proven very hard to get in touch with long distance, and I couldn't seem to catch him in person, either.

I was frustrated, and I knew I wasn't doing a very good job with this, but I had set the money aside and I wanted to see the project through. I talked with John Van Keppel, who lives in Antigua and works with an excellent organization called Child Aid. John has been an invaluable resource in this work, and in the last decade he has also become a real friend. On my next trip to the country, he picked me up in his truck and we headed for the school.

When we arrived this time, my jaw dropped. I was amazed to find that there was a whole new school there: large, two stories, and well-built. Kids were running around, and workers were finishing up final bits of construction. A teacher came out to greet us and ask if he could help, and we had a bit of a look around. After the trip, I needed a restroom, and I found a beautiful and clean one waiting inside.

What had been done here was far beyond anything PEG could have accomplished, and I was thrilled for the kids in that little town. We don't have any turf issues; it was great that more had been done by someone else than we could have done ourselves.

But I also felt pretty stupid. My own cultural illiteracy and incompetence with international communication efforts had blown this project after I had invited other people to be a part of it. They had been excited to have this direct impact, and I had not managed to make it happen. The money they had donated would go to other worthy projects, but I hadn't delivered what I said I would.

As I look back, I wonder if it might not have ultimately served the school poorly if we had come through. I have no way of actually knowing, of course, but perhaps the larger organization with better funding would have seen less need if those two basic problems had been addressed.

What I do know is that this initial project which never happened has led to over a dozen other projects, including a literacy project in partnership with Child Aid that has touched thousands of children's lives, Nino's school in Tzanchaj, significant book purchases and other improvements to several libraries in various villages, support of several different existing schools, and even a school band in the village of El Tejar. My initial bumbling led to so many other good things. That was not the last time I would blow it in this or any other part of my life, but getting it wrong may have been the best thing I could have done.

As I mentioned earlier, there has been a bit of a trend recently of books critiquing aid work. It's a good trend, on the whole, as there is much to be learned about how to do this work in ways that nurture dignity on all sides rather than destroying it on all sides. There is no question that it is entirely possible to do more harm than good and to feed destructive stereotypes and practices that wound everyone involved, especially when we fail to keep in view the values that should guide us.

> Doing it badly, while not what we should aim for, is sometimes the only way we can learn to do it better.

My concern about the trend, though, is that it will feed into the already powerful temptation to dismiss and simply stop supporting constructive efforts that are admittedly flawed, as if they or any other human effort could ever be perfect. This kind of work is inherently messy. Doing it badly, while not what we should aim for, is sometimes the only way we can learn to do it better. Accountability is good. I'm not suggesting that we should overlook significant issues with bad models of aid work, but I am suggesting that our best response is usually to improve them rather than discard them, and to have realistic expectations regarding the nature of this work.

In reality, the best of projects have negative consequences and the worst likely have some positives. Because we want to minimize the negative impact, we need to carefully study and consider our values, approaches and methods, to listen more than we speak, to learn from the people we are working with—especially people who are generally thought of as being 'served'—and to engage with mentors who have deeper knowledge and understanding of a given situation than we do, many of whom we are likely to find in the 'served' population.

But then we have to show up and get to work. If we wait until we completely understand the issues, the people, the culture, ourselves... we will wait forever. There is a balance to be struck between due diligence and engagement, and I fear that many of us err on the side of what Paul Loeb calls the 'perfect standard,' waiting until we understand everything before we do anything. That's problematic, because if we wait until we have it all figured out, we will wait forever.

Our ability to dismiss flawed (i.e. *all*) positive efforts takes us back to the two parts of the hero game: first, lionizing our heroes as different from us and therefore dismissing our own responsibilities because they are heroes and we're not; and conversely, discovering our heroes' human flaws and dismissing their efforts because we reject them as charlatans and hypocrites. We do the same thing with movements and actions that we do with individuals, and in both cases, we find ways to abdicate our responsibility to each other.

We do the same thing with movements and actions that we do with individuals, and in both cases, we find ways to abdicate our responsibility to each other.

In her fascinating book *Being Wrong*, Kathryn Schulz writes about how we view our capacity to make mistakes:

> *Of all the things we are wrong about, this idea of error might well top the list. It is our meta-mistake: we are wrong about what it means to be wrong. Far from being a sign of intellectual inferiority, the capacity to err is crucial to human cognition. Far from being a moral flaw, it is inextricable from some of our most humane and honorable qualities: empathy, optimism, imagination, conviction, and courage. And far from being a mark of indifference and intolerance, wrongness is a vital part of how we learn and change.*

Blowing it is not part of most people's picture of bringing about positive change. We expect effective world changers *not* to blow it. They (we) all do, though, and this may be another point to pay attention to when we consider our own capacity to have a positive influence. It is so easy to dismiss our own capacity to be effective because we know how flawed we are. We often forget, however, that all of the people we respect and admire are flawed, too.

Making a mistake should not be the end of your effort. It's just step one. It's joining the ranks of all people in every time and place who work for positive change. We all fall from time to time, even when we're stumbling toward the light.

Performing with friends from El Tejar, Guatemala at the LEAF festival.
(photo by David Simchock)

What Is Yours
To Do?

CHAPTER TWELVE

Discerning Your Call

I have ceased to question stars and books;
I have begun to listen to the teachings
my blood whispers to me.

— Hermann Hesse

This book is not intended to be guilt inducing. The point is not to convince you that you're not doing enough, but to clear some obstacles from your path if you're feeling a tug to contribute in ways that you haven't before. I meet a lot of people who are feeling that tug but don't know where to start. This is an effort to help with that particular quandary.

I also meet a lot of people who are completely overwhelmed by personal responsibilities, though, and I want to be abundantly clear that those count too. If you have a sick parent or child you need to care for, or if you feel called to some other very personal work, that matters.

I wear a necklace most days that jewelry artist Melissa Lowery made for me by hand. It bears Gandhi's famous dictum that I quoted a few chapters ago: "Be the change you wish to see in the world." My hope is that hanging those words around my neck will remind me of that important wisdom from time to time so that, eventually, it might sink in.

You may want to live in a world where people stand up for each other in the face of oppression. But if you also want to live in a world where people take care of their families, then perhaps your deepest call, at least for right now, is to help create that world by caring for your own family. Maybe that in itself is your movement. It is for you to decide what you need to be working on right now, and no one else.

That said, if you are feeling a tug, listen.

It can be hard to speak of 'calling' and 'vocation' in a secular context. They are inherently spiritual terms, and for my part, I understand them that way. It's not my intention to proselytize, though, and I hope that if you understand them differently, you will be willing and able to translate the ideas into your own cosmology and that they will still have some relevance for you. Whether you conceive of that call as coming from some form of God, destiny, or your own inner wisdom, I am convinced that each of us is repeatedly called and that if we can be intentional and quiet enough to listen, we will hear.

The following chapters explore some questions that I find useful when trying to discern what I am called to in a particular time and place, along with some questions that are common, but not so useful. Some may strike a chord with you; others may not. Ask what feels right and listen to what you hear. I firmly believe that this kind of discernment leads us to work that is ours to do.

CHAPTER THIRTEEN

What's Most Important?

*We cannot declare a happenstance 'just a coincidence'
without looking at whether it corresponds to a theme
or an issue in our lives.*

— Gregg Levoy

I don't think my friend Patrick was put on the earth for the purpose of telling me I'm not bad as a bar singer. But I have to admit that it changed my life back in the late eighties. His casual comment indicating some modicum of respect for my ability to make music opened me up to considering new possibilities, and that led to a long and personally nourishing career as a musician. My career led to my meeting my wife Deanna (at a concert), and that led to our honeymoon in Guatemala. Our honeymoon led to founding our non-profit, which led in turn to some Guatemalan children being able to read who might not be able to otherwise. That led to my being considered for the Rotary Peace Fellowship, which led us to move to Australia, then India. And now, it has led me to writing this book, along with many other outcomes. It's hard to overestimate the potential significance of a small action.

That said, I'm quite sure that comment wasn't a hugely significant moment in Patrick's life. It was one of innumerable moments that had innumerable effects. I had a young woman come up to me at a concert at Hendrix College in Arkansas a few years ago and tell me that she was leaving the next month for a stint in the Peace Corps. I celebrated that with her, then she looked me in the eye and said, "I'm going because I saw you in concert a couple of years ago."

I don't know what her experience was like in the Peace Corps or how she touched others' lives while she was there, but I suspect she did some good work. She seemed like someone who would. I certainly don't take credit for her choices, which were doubtless the result of many other factors and decisions, any more than Patrick accepts the weight of my decision to become a musician, nor should he. It's nice to think I played a part in there somewhere, though. And it's good to be reminded of small callings and our ability to be, as my friend Chuck Brodsky sings, 'each other's angels'.

In discussions of calling, it is natural to look for a Great Purpose in our lives. It would be wonderful to search for and discover a sense of Why We're Here. But here's a surprise:

I don't think you have a calling.

I don't think there is a reason why you're on the planet. I think there are lots of them.

That may seem like a trivial distinction, but it is not. Some people may seem to have a dominant wave in their lives, while others throw a lot of smaller ripples, but the search for our Great Life's Calling can easily become discouraging and self-defeating. It seems to me that biting off some chewable pieces right now is a much more productive approach.

I spend a fair amount of time on college campuses, between speaking and performing, and I often encounter students who are anxious about what to do after graduation. That's natural, given that it's the first time in many college students' lives that their next steps aren't somewhat scripted. I love to remind them, as they plan those next steps, that they don't have to figure it all out right now. 'What am I supposed to do with my life?' is not really a useful question; the enormity of it is overwhelming and immobilizing. A better question may be, 'What do I do next?' That's much more manageable, and much more realistic as well, given that the average person in the U.S. now has several careers over the course of their lives. Not jobs, but careers—whole different vocational trajectories.

Even a larger-than-life historical figure like Martin Luther King, Jr., didn't start off with a vision to lead the Civil Rights Movement. When he went to Birmingham, Dr. King was taking a job as the pastor of a church, or 'accepting a call', as church people put it. He showed up to do what was calling to him at that time.

When Rosa Parks was arrested, fifty-one pastors met in a church basement to discuss how they would respond. The young Dr. King was elected to the leadership of that group, the Montgomery Improvement Association. He accepted that responsibility, and history took a significant turn.

But he didn't go to Montgomery looking for that. He was invited into that work, and he showed up, after choosing first to show up for the work of being a pastor.

In a world full of significant issues, if we want to make a contribution, how do we decide? Of course we don't want to waste our time and effort. We want to have a significant impact on something that matters. How do we choose where to put our energy? What is *most* important?

'What am I supposed to do with my life?' is not really a useful question.

I have been in gatherings of activists where our energy seemed to turn on each other. People who are passionately drawn to some work in the world naturally feel its significance deeply, and it is easy to round the dangerous corner of trying to denigrate the work that others are doing in order to demonstrate the importance of your own cause. It can go roughly like this (with, admittedly, a bit of exaggeration in this rendition... but not much):

A: "So what are you working on these days?"

B: "I'm working on women's issues. I can't believe there is still massive pay inequity for the same work, and that women are so under-represented in leadership roles, so that's where I'm putting my energy. What about you?"

A: "That's great, I guess, but I'm working on animal rights issues. It seems like it's more important to speak for those who have no voices."

C: (joining the conversation) "That's fine, I guess, but with all due respect, poisoned water is an issue for everyone: male, female, human, or not. We've got to be putting our energy into challenging hydrofracturing."

D: "Well that's important too, I guess, but your local clean water issue isn't going to matter much if the whole planet melts because of global climate change! Isn't that a bit parochial?"

E: "People, we *don't have time* for the planet to melt! There are thousands of nuclear warheads rusting all over Eastern Europe, and all of ours are still set to respond on a hair trigger! If those things fall into the wrong hands, or some little wire falls against another one, it's all over!"

...and so on (I'm sure you could fill in more issues and more reasons why they are the most important), until they have worked all the way around the circle and get back to where they started:

B: "...and all those issues you are talking about? That's why we need to get more women into the conversation!"

Everyone has a reasonably sound argument. Each can present compelling reasons why his or her issue matters most. And they're all right, at least from a certain perspective. Those of us who are passionate about an issue or cause naturally want to recruit others to it. But it may not be productive or correct to assume that everyone ought to be on board with our issue. Looking at the list in the facetious conversation above, it would be tragic if everyone else was convinced by any one of the activists! What if all of them decided to work exclusively on just one of those issues while completely ceding all of the others? Even if we ignored all of the issues *but* one above, no matter which one, we would still be in trouble.

You may be thinking, "But if they're all important, do I have to work on all of them?" There is so much that needs attention, not only 'issues', but work and laundry and family and rest. Our email inboxes are full of requests for one cause or another, and it all seems to matter, but we know we can't do it all. Where do we start? And where do we draw the line?

Noam Chomsky, the famous linguist and activist, talking with Bill Moyers about his decision to speak out against the Vietnam

War, confessed his own fears along those lines, "I remember thinking hard about whether to get involved because I knew exactly where it was going to go. It's the kind of involvement which only grows. There are more issues and more problems and more needs, and once you are willing to take what is clearly the step that honesty and integrity require and become involved in these issues, there's never going to be any end to the demands."

'Compassion fatigue' is a concept that was introduced several years ago and is now quite well-documented. It's no wonder that people grow frustrated and tired of activism, if this is our context and our experience. If caring is equivalent to taking personal responsibility to work on every issue that needs someone's attention, we are doomed to discouragement, failure, and depression.

It seems to me, though, that this is another place where a shift in the question might help. Maybe, rather than, 'What is most important?', the more useful question to ask is, 'What am *I* called to work on?'

CHAPTER FOURTEEN

What's Bugging You?

*If you are neutral in situations of injustice, you have chosen
the side of the oppressor. If an elephant has its foot on
the tail of a mouse and you say that you are neutral,
the mouse will not appreciate your neutrality.*

— Desmond Tutu

My son's name is Mason. We named him that for a few reasons, but primarily because we hope he will grow up to be someone who builds, like a stone mason, rather than someone who tears down. The time goes quickly, as most parents will attest. He is now five and excited to begin kindergarten in the fall. Homework is a fascinating and exciting concept for him, and we are not discouraging that perception.

Though he is changing quickly, it is still not hard to remember when he was three. As three-year-olds go, he was a gentle and easy kid, remarkably empathic for such a little guy, and fun to be with. But still three.

Much of what we think of as 'the Terrible Twos' actually happens in the early threes, I think, in the same way that much of what we think of as 'the sixties' actually happened in the early seventies. We're funny about time.

My wife Deanna read somewhere recently that the hormone swings in three-year-old boys are more drastic than in fourteen-year-old boys, and I believe it. Deanna was singing with him while he took a bath one night, and she sang a line from a song that he thought had different words. His face contorted in tears of protest.

In those days, he had also not yet mastered the skill of taking turns in conversation. If Deanna was talking, he would, in classic style, tug on her pants and say, "Mommy... Mommy... Mommy...

Mommy... Mommy... Mommy... Mommy! Mommy! Mommy! Mommy! MOMMY! MOMMY!" Luckily, whatever he wanted to say was usually pretty interesting.

Sometimes a calling is like that: it drives you nuts. And I don't just mean that it is persistent. I mean that it is annoying.

We tend to think of callings in grand, slow-motion, cinematic terms, with strings swelling in the background and a beam of sunlight breaking through the clouds. Burning bushes and mountaintops and such.

> *Sometimes a calling is like that: it drives you nuts. And I don't just mean that it is persistent. I mean that it is annoying.*

Sometimes, though, our proverbial pants legs are tugged by what I have come to think of as *negative callings* rather than *positive callings*. The latter draw you into something because it looks exciting or calls for your gifts, like my decision to have a go at playing music professionally.

The negative callings, on the other hand, are in response to something that isn't right. We perceive the injustice and we feel called to do something about it, to engage in changing it. Callings can come in the form of frustration as easily as positive inspiration. Both are legitimate, although the negative ones are a bit less romantic.

If you were old enough and were in the U.S. at the time, you may remember that during the run-up to the Iraq war, there was a proliferation of bumper stickers that said 'God Bless America'. Denotatively, I can get behind that statement. It squares with my faith (and it is specifically a faith-based statement). Yes, please, God continue to bless America, which I'm pretty sure means the United States in this case (though I have met people from several other countries in North, Central, and South America who take exception to that usage—they're Americans too).

And that's part of the point. The statement leaves me uncomfortable because it is conspicuous in who it leaves out. Plus, it's not theologically or rationally sound to recruit God to our priorities. If we're bringing God into it, we need to go with God's priorities, which, according to my own tradition (and many others say the same thing in other words), include loving your enemies and praying for those who persecute you. So a more faithful bumper sticker would perhaps have read 'God Bless Iraq', even if we felt convinced that Iraq was our enemy, a conclusion I question, but won't take on here.

Of course, putting *that* on my car would have accomplished little other than supporting the local window repair business. I was talking about this with my parents in their living room one day, and I said, "Somebody ought to make a bumper sticker that says *God bless every nation*. That's not quite as confrontational, and it might make people think about it a bit—maybe even notice the contrast between the two and have to consider which of those ideas they subscribe to."

Then I smiled and groaned, realizing what I had done. It's always dangerous to say the words, "Somebody ought to...." I realized that I knew how to design and order bumper stickers; I had done it before as a musician. When we hear ourselves say "Somebody ought to..." we run the risk of remembering that we are somebody. My dad offered the wise amendment that perhaps it should say 'God bless *the people* of every nation', so as to differentiate between people and their governments.

I had the stickers made, gave away a bunch of them, and when I could no longer afford that, sold many more. Now I've distributed well over 10,000 of them at concerts and through my own web site. When another company called to see whether I would allow them to use the design, I said, "Sure, no charge, no problem." Mostly I just wanted to get that message out. I have no idea how many more they have distributed.

I don't know what effect this has had, of course, but I would like to think that it has contributed to some significant conversations, whether internal or external. If it resonates for you, then you feel a bit less alone at a time and place where your opinion is not mainstream. If it annoys you, vaguely or explicitly, you at least need to take a moment to consider why, and whether your logic holds up. That's all I hoped for, and I think it has happened. And it was born of my frustration. It arose out of a "Somebody ought to..." statement.

Could I have spent my time and money on something more important than making bumper stickers? Well, maybe. I'm sure someone could make a reasonable argument that I could have. I tend to think, though, that that was my particular calling on that particular day.

That proverbial tug on her pants leg led to a whole career.

I would not have gotten to it by asking, 'What is my Life's Great Calling?' Rather, I had to engage the question, 'What is calling to me today?' Once I realized that I knew how to get bumper stickers made and that this was tugging on me, it was pretty clearly mine to do.

My sister Kathy has led an extremely diverse professional life, including being a professional potter, running a shoe store, and even working with me for a while, handling my booking and office management. In her forties, she became increasingly concerned about and engaged with our broken death penalty system. Finally, she decided that she needed to go to law school. She began Cornell at age fifty and is now practicing as a death penalty defense attorney in North Carolina. She likes to joke that she got her student ID card and her AARP card in the mail in the same month. That proverbial tug on her pants leg led to a whole career.

Of course, positive callings count too. The corollary question to 'What's bugging you?' is 'What inspires you?' What do you see happening in the world that makes you sit up a bit straighter and feel a little more hopeful about the human race?

For my mother in the eighties, that was Habitat for Humanity. She ended up giving seven years of full-time volunteer work, founding and chairing the local chapter in Roanoke, Virginia. It was a great deal of work, but it brought her great joy, and that chapter has now built over 200 houses for people with low income to buy at reasonable prices with no interest loans. Habitat relies heavily on volunteer labor—hundreds of thousands of people pitching in a few days of dedication and 'sweat equity'. It is a massive movement built from the accumulation of many people's time and energy, donated because they see something good happening and they want to be a part of it.

In response to both kinds of callings, negative and positive, the next question is 'What small thing can you do about it?' How do we move from applauding something someone else is doing to doing some of those things ourselves? Conversely, how do we work to impede the things that seem wrong to us?

Ask yourself those questions, not in the abstract, but specifically. What's bugging *you*? What inspires *you*? What small thing can *you* do about it? There's no telling where the answers to those questions might lead.

CHAPTER FIFTEEN

What Do You Bring?

Talent is like electricity.
We don't understand electricity.
We use it.

— Maya Angelou

So how do you go about making a difference?

Get a job working for US Airways at the Guatemala City airport. I'd say that's the best way.

At least it was in June of 2008, when I found myself delayed in Guatemala due to an equipment malfunction on a US Airways jet. Airplanes are complicated machines, and it is the nature of machines to malfunction sometimes, so I was grateful that we were delayed overnight rather than flying on a plane with a maintenance issue.

The timing, however, was significantly problematic for me. I was returning from a trip to Guatemala in which I'd traveled by all manners of transportation imaginable, from motorcycle taxi to boat to the back of a passing pick up truck to a 'chicken bus' (retired school buses from the U.S., so named because you may well find yourself sitting next to a bag of chickens, and also because the bus drivers play chicken with each other while passing each other on the winding mountain roads, getting out of the oncoming lane just in time, or sometimes almost in time).

I was planning to fly home to North Carolina that night, drop off my grubby clothes, pick up my suit and guitar, and fly immediately to California, where I was scheduled to be a breakfast keynote speaker the following morning for the biennial General Assembly of the Presbyterian Church (U.S.A.).

Melissa Gutierrez, an employee at the Guatemala City

airport, came to me at the end of a very long line (read: the entire plane) of unhappy passengers, greeted me with a smile, and proceeded to spend a full thirty minutes working on finding some way to get me to California in time for my talk. At no time did her good attitude waver, in spite of the fact that, as I learned later, she was on the end of a fourteen-hour-plus work day, and I had just watched her dealing with several extremely unpleasant customers who seemed to hold her personally responsible for the equipment problem.

Most of the three previous paragraphs are taken directly from a letter I wrote to US Airways after that experience. When I began my talk in California early in the morning of the following day, I started the hour I had been allotted by thanking Melissa Gutierrez in absentia and expressing my gratitude that not everyone who is compassionate and generous of spirit goes into the ministry.

Want to have a positive impact and make good things happen? Get a job working for US Airways. Or you could become a Certified Public Accountant.

At least that's one way. My friend Katherine Neville is one. She's good at it. She likes putting the numerical pieces of the puzzle together and coming up with something that makes sense and doesn't have any bits sticking out. Me? Not so much.

But I have a passion for Guatemalan children having a shot at education, so I have a small non-profit, PEG Partners, as I described earlier. Because Katherine believes in that cause and has this particular gift to bring, she has been the treasurer and CPA for PEG for ten years now. She has contributed immensely, and I can't imagine what we would have done without her.

I'm sure you see where I'm going with this. There are many kinds of callings and many ways to contribute. Two of the helpful questions we can ask ourselves in an effort to determine what we will work on next have to do with what we bring as particular individuals. What do you bring?

That's a pretty general question, but it bears some thought. To narrow it down, it may be helpful to ask a couple of other questions as well. The first one is, 'What are you good at?' What can you do that not everyone can do?

The second is, 'What do you love doing?' The answers may not not always the same thing, but they can both be enlightening questions to ask when you are considering your vocation (in the sense of 'calling' rather than 'job'). Your skills, whatever they may be, are needed somewhere. Really.

Howard Thurman, an author, philosopher, and preacher who was a mentor to Martin Luther King, Jr., said, "Don't just ask what the world needs. Ask what makes you come alive and then go and do it, because what the world needs is people who have come alive." That may not be universally applicable, but it's a good place to start (if selling heroin really makes you happy, there may be some more questions to consider before throwing yourself fully into it, though I suspect Rev. Thurman would not consider that 'coming alive' in a deep sense).

You may be thinking that what you love has no place in service. If so, I would encourage you to think a bit more about it before letting the idea go.

I got an email from a student named Eric Keen a few years ago. He wrote that he had seen a concert of mine the summer before and had been thinking a lot about some things I had shared during the concert, including the Howard Thurman quote I mention above. Eric said that at first it hadn't seemed like those words applied to him.

Eric explained that he and his best friend Jason had a passion for cycling. When they weren't riding bikes they were talking about them, working on them, researching them, etc. Cycling is not a destructive hobby, but the primary benefits seemed for the most part to be personal. It didn't burn fossil fuels and it developed their own health, but they didn't see a proactive generosity in it. How could riding their bikes be of service to others?

As they talked about it, though, an idea began to emerge. If they cycled across Canada and took pledges for their adventure, they could raise money, have a fun summer, and spend a *lot* of time riding their bikes. In the summer of 2008 they did just that, and they raised over $14,000 for a school in Chacaya, Guatemala, a small coffee-growing village on Lago Atítlan. In cooperation with another organization, Sharing the Dream, the local Parents' Committee and community leaders had raised money to buy some land and move their school out of a rented space with walls made of loosely woven reeds, and they had asked PEG Partners if we could help build the school. Eric and Jason made a huge contribution to that effort—and had a whole lot of fun doing it.[24] I have visited the school several times since then, and I can testify to the positive effect it has had on the children to be in a sturdy, safe, and clean building.

Too often, we think that if we're not miserable, we're not trying hard enough, not answering our most 'noble' call. However, I think Howard Thurman is closer to the truth; if our work is making us miserable, it may not be our deepest call. On the other hand, if it is making us 'come alive', that may be a clue that we're on the right track.

That's not to say that good work doesn't require sacrifice and courage. Clearly, it requires both, and sometimes in large measure. Reading Civil Rights hero John Lewis' autobiography, *Walking With the Wind*, it is hard not to be overwhelmed by the suffering that he and his companions willingly chose to endure in order to reveal and challenge the injustice of racism.

You may be thinking that what you love has no place in service. If so, I would em you to think a bit more about it before letting the idea go.

"Faith contains a certain ferocity," writes Gregg LeVoy in his book *Callings*, "an unspoken demand that to maintain it we part ways with comfort and give up something we have for something we want. We may have to relinquish the precious commodities of time and energy, or something that represents security to us, or simply whatever internal resistance stands in our way." LeVoy is right. Sometimes worldchanging requires stepping beyond comfort and even safety. But we should be careful to distinguish between

---

[24] Jason and Eric published a book about that summer: http://bit.ly/1kemtGZ

the idea that courage and service sometimes require suffering and the idea that suffering is noble in and of itself. Our joy can also be of service, and that kind of service tends to be more sustainable.

Lewis and his friends were willing to relinquish even their personal safety for some other things they wanted: freedom and equality. I've had the privilege of spending a bit of time talking with John Lewis, though, and I can attest to the fact that, even in the face of the great sacrifices he has made, his work has unquestionably made him 'come alive'. He is quick to smile and laugh, and no stranger to joy.

Looking for where your joy lies may be a good place to start in terms of seeking your place in the movement to make the world a better place. It is also important, though, to look at the particular skills and resources you bring.

My friend David Gill runs a camp on the outskirts of Little Rock, Arkansas.

We should be careful to distinguish between the idea that courage and service sometimes require suffering and the idea that suffering is noble in and of itself.

Ferncliff is, in some ways, a fairly typical summer camp and conference center, with a fishing pond, hiking trails, a swimming pool, and campfires. It is a beautiful and peaceful place and has given the essential gifts of rest and retreat to generations of people.

In March of 1998, there was a school shooting just outside Jonesboro, Arkansas. Four young children and one teacher were killed, and ten others were wounded. David Gill thought that after some time had passed, the surviving children might benefit from a camp experience. He made discreet inquiries to gauge interest, made the invitation, and began raising the money needed to provide that service for free.

Gill assembled a team that included psychologists who trained the camp staff and counselors and were available to the students while they were there. The camp was a powerful and fun experience for the kids. It was not designed to force them to deal with their traumatic experience, but simply to have a healthy retreat experience, with appropriate resources available if they were needed.

After the first year, it was clear that there was deep value in this experience, and the various people involved decided to continue to invite these middle school children back each year until they graduated from high school. It turned out to be eight camps over five years. I was invited as a concert artist for several of those years, and one year I was asked to teach a creative writing class as well. I led a corporate writing process with the students that involved generating and choosing a topic together, and the kids chose to write about watching Saturday morning cartoons in sock footed pajamas. These kids were not defined by their trauma, and the camp was, to some degree, a vehicle for them to resist that definition.

Then the story took a turn that no one could have anticipated. Just over a year later, in 1999, there was another school shooting, this time in Columbine, Colorado. Naturally, the children from Jonesboro were deeply affected by this news, and their response was to reach out to the students from Columbine. Adults helped facilitate a connection (though the idea came from the students themselves), and some of the Jonesboro kids, being among the few people who actually knew how it felt to go through such a thing, traveled to meet with survivors of the Columbine shooting. Later, they invited them to be a part of the camp experience at Ferncliff, and some came. Eventually, the kids even invited children from Sarajevo, who had survived the violence of the Bosnian war, to join them as well.

David Gill set in motion an extraordinary cascade of healing influence in the face of tragic situations by bringing his particular gifts and the resources of the camp. Later, the Jonesboro students brought the gift of their own experience to the service of others in pain. They brought their gifts, their identity, their passion, and their history to their service.

It may be helpful to further break down the question of what you bring; it is not only a question of what you love. What you bring also includes elements of who you are (which we will look at in a later chapter), the various resources you have access to, and the skills you have developed by living your particular life.

The question of what you're good at is sometimes a separate question from that of what you love. There may be times when you are called to offer something that doesn't in and of itself 'make you come alive,' but is nonetheless an essential way to truly support something you care about with a gift that only you can bring. Being asked to contribute a certain skill to a cause you believe in when that skill is not common may be another sign that this work is for you. What is *particularly* yours to contribute?

My friend Hugh Hollowell, as I mentioned earlier, leads an organization called Love Wins in Raleigh, North Carolina, that nurtures community with people who don't have housing. He told me the story of a volunteer who showed up one day, asking what he could do to help out. Hugh asked him what he did for a day job and the volunteer responded that he was an I.T. guy. Hugh said, "Great! We've actually got issues with both of our computers! Can you take a look?" The guy responded that he would really rather do something else, since he does that all day at work.

Hugh, a Mennonite pastor, almost renounced his commitment to nonviolence.

I.T. work, apparently, was not where this volunteer found joy, but it was a skill that was desperately needed, and one that he had to offer. If he wanted to be of service that day, rather than simply have a day off, offering that skill would have been the best way to do it. Not for the rest of his life, perhaps, but certainly for this one day.

When Deanna, Mason (then just turning one), and I moved to India in 2009, I packed my boots and gloves. Just a few weeks before, there had been terrible flooding in the part of the country where we were headed, and the organization I was going to be working for, Arthik Samata Mandal (ASM), does disaster relief work as well as sustainable development.

When I got there, however, I found that most of the clean up work was already done. More importantly, I realized how silly I had been to think that manual labor would be a helpful contribution for me to make. There are some shortages in rural India, but manual labor is not one of them. It's not a particularly strong skill for me at home, either, so why would it be the gift I bring in India?

In fact, I found that what the organization needed from me was in another skill area altogether. ASM is good at the work they do, which has largely evolved from cleaning up disasters to sustainable development—making communities stronger in the first place, so that they can better withstand disasters when they occur.

> There are some shortages in rural India, but manual labor is not one of them.

They were finding it challenging, however, to tell their story, especially to westerners. What they needed, it turns out, were some brochures. I had enough basic skill in photography, copywriting, and layout and design to give them something useful, especially for a western audience. They requested that I create brochures for three of their flagship programs, so I designed, wrote, and shot photos to tell those stories and give the basic information and rationale for each. This served me well as field research for my masters program because I got to know those programs intimately, did a lot of travel into the field, conducted interviews, and shot over 4,000 pictures, all of which was both academically engaging and a personal joy to me. I supported the organization in other ways while I was there, as well, but the research and design was my primary responsibility.

It's not nearly as glamorous, of course, as slogging through mud to pull people to safety, but it was what was really needed from me. That can be another useful questions to ask ourselves. What is actually needed from me in this situation?

We have the same attitude with PEG, as we try to meet real needs that are driven by circumstances in particular Guatemalan communities rather than donor preferences. Recently, we helped fund a construction project at an overcrowded school in Pachaj, Cantel, in the Quetzalenango province of Guatemala. We were

Change Agent training in Srikakulam for young women from nearby villages

originally planning to help fund one of the classrooms, but when the project began, the school officials came back to us and asked if they could use our money to fund a strong cement and steel railing around the whole area, something that would be a significant contribution to the children's safety. It doesn't sound nearly as cool to say that we funded the construction of a railing as it does to say that we funded the construction of a classroom, but it was what was really needed, and our goal is to be of real service, not just service that sounds good.

This question of 'what you bring' came to me in stark relief this year when I was arrested for the second time in my life, as part of the Moral Mondays movement here in North Carolina, again in the state legislative building. This time I was arrested for second degree trespassing (in a public building), and for some version of disturbing the peace, which included 'loud singing'. I'm particularly proud of that charge, though the truth is I'm a rather quiet singer. I never would have made it in the days before microphones.

It occurred to me at one point how glad I was that my lawyer had not chosen to be arrested, since he would then not be allowed to do the work he was doing. Likewise, it is good that I was not called on to do his job, as I know very little about law. I'm also deeply grateful for the people who brought sandwiches to the church where we all gathered in the middle of the night when we were released, and to the people playing guitars, singing, and laughing in that fellowship hall. It was incredibly cleansing to have their joy and their music wash over us after being in jail.

But calling is not always about 'issues', either. Sometimes we are called to care for the people around us in particular ways that only we are suited for.

> *Sometimes we are called to care for the people around us in particular ways that only we are suited for.*

In the last few pages of Rosa Parks' autobiography she off-handedly writes these words about the period after her husband died from cancer in 1977,

> *Mama was ill with cancer too, and after my husband died, I had to put her in a nursing home for a year, because I wasn't able to give her the proper care and work too. But I visited her for breakfast, lunch, and dinner every day, seven days a week.*

As she often did, Rosa Parks sets quite a high bar for the rest of us, but I think it's notable that this deeply committed, legendary activist, named by *Time Magazine* as one of the hundred most influential people of her century, prioritized her family. There is no compromise in that.

No one has the authority or the knowledge to tell you what you are or are not called to do. It is a deeply personal question, and it requires courageous self-examination and deep listening. If you are feeling tugged to engage in ways that you haven't before, to reach outside of your immediate circle of comfort, there may be something you need to pay attention to in that.

Sometimes, I should say, the gift you bring is not specific to you. These questions are not the only ones that help discern call. In the Moral Mondays protests that have been taking place here in North Carolina, what is often needed is simply more warm bodies standing together at the legislature. Just being present is actually huge contribution.

If there is one thing I hope to get across in these pages, though, it is that the most significant work is often the least dramatic. Do the thing that is yours to do in this moment. And if your body and spirit are telling you that your highest call right now is to nourish and heal yourself, then please do that. We need you for the long haul, and when you are ready for the next thing, I trust that you will feel that tug.

You're still reading, though, so maybe you're already feeling it.

CHAPTER SIXTEEN

Personal Sustainability

To allow oneself to be carried away by a multitude of conflicting concerns, to surrender to too many demands, to commit oneself to too many projects, to want to help everyone in everything, is to succumb to violence.

— Thomas Merton

When I was a child, more than a few well-intentioned adults told me that if I worked hard enough and made good decisions, I could do anything I wanted to. I just had to set my mind to it and get to work.

The problem is, that's not true.

If, for instance, I decided today that I am going to devote the rest of my life to being a professional NBA basketball player, it's still not going to happen. Even if I had decided that as a child, my NBA career would still have been unlikely. I don't have the right body for it. We all have limitations, and those limitations are as unique to each of us as our gifts are.

I don't think those kind caretakers intended to lie to me; I think they hadn't thought it through. They were offering a simplified version of the truth, and—like the simplified version of the Rosa Parks arrest story—at some point, when we simplify a story too much, it stops being true. We don't serve our kids well by telling them things that sound encouraging but aren't true.

The truth I believe they were aiming for is this: Almost everyone on the planet, very likely including you, is capable of much, much more than we think we are capable of. The main obstacle in our way is a belief in limitations that do not, in fact, exist.

That's a more complex idea, but it has the added benefit of actually being true.

Each of us has real limits regarding not only our capacity, but also how much we can take on at any given time. And to up the proverbial ante, it is also true that if you take a step toward involvement in something that matters to you, it is likely that your awareness will increase and you will drop some of your defenses regarding getting involved with *other* things that *also* matter to you. Before you know it, you may find that you have your time, money, and emotional energy invested in so many causes that you can't seem to remember the passion that got you involved in the first place. So how do you cope with that overload?

The world needs a few martyrs from time to time, but very few.

This question matters a great deal. 'No' is not my specialty, and I often find myself over-committed as a result. I think I'm getting better, though. The best path toward sane and sustainable contribution that I've found is to keep returning to the question of what is for *me* to do, rather than what is *important* in a general sense. This is an important part of discerning what we are called to work on—discerning what we are *not* called to work on, as worthy as the cause may be.

It's OK, when a zealous friend is trying to recruit you to their cause, to say, "That's important, and I'm cheering you on as you work on it, but it's not mine to do right now. I am committed to some other things that are also important." I recall offering some version of that response to a friend who was asking for my help within the last year. He smiled and said, "Okay. I'm an organizer. It's my job to ask, and it's your job to say yes or no."

That wasn't too hard. Burning out from overcommitment is not a sustainable strategy, and the most effective activists know this.

I've been happy to see the term 'personal sustainability' gaining ground in activist circles in recent years. The fundamental question this concept raises is, 'How can you take care of yourself so that you can continue to contribute?' That is a very different model from the model of martyrdom: sacrificing yourself for the cause.

As we discussed earlier, that's not to say that effective worldchanging doesn't sometimes include real and even painful sacrifice. As the stories of John Lewis, Nelson Mandela, and other notable worldchangers demonstrate, sometimes it does. If it is all sacrifice and no joy, however, you will have a hard time sticking with it for long.

The world needs a few martyrs from time to time, but very few. Personal sustainability allows you to *keep* contributing, which, in the long run, is usually a better deal for both you and the world around you.

CHAPTER SEVENTEEN

The Power In
Who You Are

So the rose is its own credential,
a certain unattainable effortless form:
wearing its heart visibly,
it gives us heart too:
bud, fulness and fall.

— *Daniel Berrigan*, from the poem "Credentials", 1957

The only time that I ever performed for a fully armed audience was in Bosnia and Herzegovina, in the year 2000.

I was heading to Europe for a concert tour, playing in a few European countries after concerts in Australia and New Zealand. Maryl Neff, a friend I knew from acoustic music circles in the United States, was working as a civilian employee for the U.S. Army, serving peacekeeping troops in Bosnia. Part of her duty included booking entertainment for the troops stationed on the base where she lived, and UN peacekeeping troops from several different countries often attended those events. When she saw that I was coming to Europe, she dropped a note to see if I wanted to come perform at Eagle Base in Tuzla. In the aftermath of the brutal Bosnian war, that area was still considered a 'hostile fire zone', so the troops were required to have firearms and ammunition with them at all times.

I tuned very carefully that night.

OK, I wasn't really worried that I would be shot. The pub on the base where I ended up performing only served non-alcoholic drinks, so, as Master Sergeant Brian O'Connors quipped, "Neither the weapons nor the troops were loaded." I had prepared myself for some ribbing, however, stepping into a military culture with my long hair and bestickered guitar case. It seemed likely that I would have some stereotyping to contend with—and as it turned out, I did.

The stereotypes I battled, however, ended up being mine rather than theirs. The audience was attentive, enthusiastic, and extremely supportive, all the while holding their rifles at their sides. After the show, several of us stood and talked for a while, and I passed my guitar around so that others could play a bit too. I'm still in touch with one soldier I met that night, who recently celebrated his retirement. The entire night, there was not a single mention of my out-of-place hairstyle. It was *I* who had unfair preconceived notions of what kind of people *they* would be, not the other way around.

Later, in Sarajevo, I connected with Dzevad Avdagic, a Muslim man who was working for the Christian organization Church World Service. Dzevad welcomed me into his home, and his kind wife fed me. I sat on his couch in the living room after dinner, drinking strong Bosnian coffee while he told me stories. At one point, I reached up to put my finger in a bullet hole in the wooden frame of his living room china cabinet; the window had long-since been repaired, but, like everywhere I turned in Sarajevo, the evidence of the war seemed inescapable. Later, when we walked to town, we stopped at a red-dyed patch of cement on his street where Dzevad had held a young girl from his neighborhood while she died from a mortar shell wound.

That evening, Dzevad and I attended what was easily the most extraordinary choir practice I have ever witnessed. The Pontanima Choir was rehearsing, and we stopped by and listened for a few songs. On the surface, there was nothing particularly amazing going on; they sang beautifully, but many choirs do. However, one incredible detail changed everything: these were Muslims, Orthodox Christians, Jews, and Catholics singing each other's sacred music together. In the immediate aftermath of a brutal war, with peacekeeping troops still on the ground and destruction all around them, these people, whose relatives had been killing and killed by each other, were standing side by side and singing together.

I can't help but believe that this courageous artistic act—

intentionally re-humanizing each other, standing and singing together and honoring each other's faith and music—accomplished more than dia-logue alone could have hoped to. The members of the Pontanima Choir have made the intentional choice to open their hearts to each other when they lift their voices together, and the music they make is transformative. They have gone on to tour around the world, singing at venues like the Kennedy Center. They not only sing their message; they embody it.

Major Walt Spangler, III carrying my guitar at the Sarajevo airport.

Ivo Markovic, the founder of the choir, tells the story of its origins, "The idea was to be a form of positive provocation. We wanted to show these religious groups, so fully enslaved to nationalism, that there is another way to be, that religions can make positive contributions."

In an article about Pontanima, Andrew Packman writes, "Markovic's vision is for a living, breathing project of reconciliation. He believes that if people learn to sing the religious other's songs of lament, praise, grief, and hope, they will have come a long way toward loving one another. And if people hardened by the war can have an experience of beauty not just in spite of but based on Bosnia's pluralism, reconciliation might just begin to take root."

It is worth noting that it is the identities of the choir members that make this such a radical act. They are drawing on the power of who they are, and the beauty they are creating is enriched by the mosaic of their diversity. By throwing out the scripts that they are expected to follow as members of different faiths and ethnicities in a war-torn country, they are choosing to use their identities to challenge the very roots of war.

The closest I have come to participating in such an event was at the Abraham Jam, an interfaith concert I organized at Duke University in 2011. At a time when Islamophobia and anti-Semitism both seemed to be on the rise, the North Carolina Council of Churches, where I was working part-time, wanted to take a strong stand of support for our interfaith colleagues. Students from all three Abrahamic faith groups and from several of the colleges in the area helped to put the event on, doing a lot of the leg work and choosing the name and the artists to perform. They wanted it to have high production values, so they sought out professional musicians. Dawud Wharnsby, a well-loved Muslim singer/songwriter, and Dan Nichols, a popular Jewish singer/songwriter, both joined me on stage, and I filled the Christian role. It was a magical night, and some time later we met up in Kalamazoo, Michigan to do it again. I am hopeful that we will have more opportunities in the future.

By throwing out the scripts that they are expected to follow as members of different faiths and ethnicities in a war-torn country, they are choosing to use their identities to challenge the very roots of war.

Because, like the Pontanima Choir, we wanted to embody our mutual respect and support and not just talk and sing about it, we chose to all be on stage together the entire night. We alternated songs rather than sets, and sometimes jumped in to sing a harmony, take a lead or play percussion on each other's songs. We invited poets of the three faiths and a dancer to join us, as well. The entire night was extraordinary.

It was an opportunity to build what we think is right, which is often the best way to oppose what we think is wrong. And it gave the community a different story to tell.

Expectations are powerful, and defying them has the potential to shock people out of their assumptions. Billionaire Warren Buffet's advocacy for raising taxes on the rich, for instance, is surprising to many people and breaks us out of the temptation to categorize the 99% as 'good' and the 1% as 'evil'. We expect the extremely rich to be opposed to more taxes for the rich, but in this case, Buffet's sense of justice triumphs over greed.

Johnny Cummings, an out gay man, serves as the mayor of Vicco, Kentucky, a small Appalachian town of about 330 people. He has strong support in the town, which in 2013 became the smallest town in the United States to pass a ban on discrimination based on gender identity or sexual orientation. Stephen Colbert ran an ironic segment called "People Who Are Destroying America" telling the story of Mayor Cummings and Vicco, KY, on his political comedy show, *The Colbert Report*. It made news because people from small Southern towns are not expected to be supportive of out gay men.

My friend Abdullah Antepli is the Muslim chaplain at Duke University and a courageous advocate of human rights for all. In the summer of 2011, he toured several African countries where there is extreme tension and frequent violence between Christians and Muslims. He traveled with a Catholic Bishop, and the two of them gave talks and led worship together for several weeks. In telling me about it, Abdullah said, "Sometimes it didn't matter what we said. It was just being seen together on the same platform, treating each other with respect. That was enough to astound people, and to change the tone." Who they were mattered as much as what they did.

So what is your own identity? Are you Southern? Are you wealthy? Are you an immigrant? Are you a veteran? Are you a member of a faith group? Are you poor? What do you care about that people might not expect you to care about? Where are you in the mainstream? Where are you on the margins? What tools does that identity afford you? There may be clues there to discerning what you might be called to work on next.

When I was about fourteen, I went to Haiti on a church mission trip. It would have been about 1982, I think. As is often the case with those kinds of trips, we did not make much of a meaningful contribution there in terms of work, but we were radically changed, or at least I was.[25]

My family lived a moderate middle-class life, by U.S. standards, and because we knew quite a lot of wealthy people, as a child I thought we were more or less poor. Although I knew something about world poverty in the abstract, I had not really come to understand my material wealth and privilege when judged on a world scale, at least not in such a tangible way.

My short trip to Haiti was an encounter with the most dire poverty I had yet seen. I came home painfully aware of my own privilege and the stark injustice of it; neither I nor the young people I met there had been given a choice as to where we would prefer to be born, but the random circumstances of our births led to much broader opportunities for me than for them. As a fourteen-year-old, I had a hard time processing that. I still do. It was one thing to theorize about it, another to spend time with real people who were just like me in so many respects—except that they were literally starving, through no fault of their own.

I have a clear memory from that trip, though I must admit that now, thirty years later, I can't swear that it actually happened. It might have been a dream I had or a memory that has morphed over time. Regardless, the point is the same, and it has become part of my story.

One day in a market in Port-au-Prince, I became separated from the rest of the group (I am naturally prone to wandering). When I tried take a shortcut to get back to them, I saw a man lying across the little side alley I needed to walk through. He was emaciated and appeared to be starving, though looking back now it is also possible that he was racked by AIDS or another illness.

---

[25] This is not the place for a detailed critique of church mission trips, but it is an important conversation to have. I recommend When Helping Hurts by Steve Corbett & Brian Fikkert as a useful tool for examining those efforts. In this context, I'm talking about the trip's effect on me, and I value that highly as I look back on my own trajectory.

The only way for me to get back to the group was to literally step over him. So I did. Even at fourteen, the metaphor was not lost on me.

It is common for people to speak of such trips by saying, "I never knew how lucky I am." That observation is a good first step, but it's not enough. If people who are privileged stop with feeling fortunate (or worse, 'blessed') because of that privilege and go on their (or our) merry way, there is a problem. To be honest with ourselves and each other, we must also acknowledge our common humanity, the injustice inherent in that unequal opportunity, and the responsibilities that come with privilege: a responsibility to work to open up opportunity where it is lacking, a responsibility to listen and learn about privilege from marginalized people who are in a better position to perceive it, and a responsibility to subvert the systems that maintain that inequality.

At fourteen, I was troubled. I was ashamed of my privilege and of my identity. I came home and wanted to give away everything I had. That was problematic, of course, since I was fourteen and didn't actually have much. It's bad form to give away your parents' stuff.

It was also a dubious proposition, though, because I *couldn't* stop being who I was, and still am. As someone pointed out in our debriefing of the trip, even if I had been standing naked and penniless in the middle of the Haitian countryside, I would still have been the wealthiest person for miles. I had U.S. citizenship, a middle school education and access to higher education, White identity, and fluent English—not to mention that I was male and straight and a member of a dominant faith group, all of which offer access that is often denied, both in my own culture and in Haiti, to people who cannot claim those identities. Though not from a family that was considered wealthy back in the United States, by Haitian standards I was unquestionably affluent. I was dealt nearly the entire hand of privilege cards.

I have continued to struggle with this experience through the years as I've returned to developing countries and spent a bit of time in places like Atlanta's Open Door Community, which is sometimes described with a wink as an 'unintentional community'. The Open Door is made up of people who were formerly homeless and people who have never been without shelter, living in solidarity and community with people who are living on the street.

Spending time with these folks in Atlanta, I was able to process my struggles with privilege a bit more. As a teenager, I had simply held onto that shame until it soaked into my skin, but as an adult, I find myself able to look more analytically at these kinds of experiences.

It has been several years now since I visited the Open Door, but I distinctly remember a piece of art hanging on the wall not too far from the front door. It holds words often attributed to Lilla Watson, an Australian Murri activist:

If you have come here to help me, you are wasting your time. But if you have come because your liberation is bound up with mine, then let us work together.[26]

Those words speak to the fact that oppression damages all of us, even the oppressors. Though everyone does not bear equal responsibility, we cannot be neatly categorized into 'victim' and 'perpetrator' when it comes to social ills, and 'helper' and 'helped' are equally unhelpful boxes in which to put people. Pity attacks dignity; it does not support it.

Likewise, a sense of existential guilt has limited usefulness. Guilt is essentially self-focused; it emphasizes our own failures and inadequacies rather than directing our attention to others to whom we have responsibilities. In the short-term, it may point us toward problems that need to be addressed, but if our sense of guilt doesn't develop into motivation for action, then it can just as easily be demoralizing and disempowering, convincing us that we are fundamentally flawed, and therefore unlikely to have any positive

---

[26] Lilla Watson, who has been, among other things, a professor at the University of Queensland where I did my graduate studies, does not claim authorship of this phrase, but says she was a part of a group that formulated it together. http://unnecessaryevils.blogspot.com/2008/11/attributing-words.html (Note: this source misspells her name as 'Lila,' but it is 'Lilla').

impact. We are unwise to indulge it because it has an inertia all its own, making objects at rest (ourselves) tend to remain at rest. And objects at rest are much less likely to change the world.

I cannot alter my fundamental identity, even if I want to, and it is wasted effort to try. More importantly, though, changing who I am is not, or at least *should* not be, my goal. My identity is part of the tool bag I have been given to work with. Rather than wishing it were otherwise, it would be more effective to see how I can use this identity in the service of justice. How can I challenge systems that offer me more power than I deserve by working in partnership with people who are denied that power? How can I use my circumstance of privilege to shine light on injustices and offer resources to those who need them? To use language discussed earlier in this book, how can I both work to meet people's needs and challenge the systems that make some of us needy?

Changing who I am is not, or at least should not be, my goal.

I've tended to fit into the demographic mainstream for most of my life, but everyone, including me, finds themselves marginalized from time to time. Sometimes we find ourselves in both the mainstream and the margin at the same moment because we have certain cultural power by one metric and not by another. Both positions offer certain tools and certain dangers, and it is worthwhile to study them and come to understand where we fit in a given context.[27]

I wrote in an earlier chapter about the night I spent in jail in May of 2011. One of the reasons I decided to take that particular stand is that I thought I could contribute something simply by being White. The issues we were challenging that day included massive cuts to education funding, voter disenfranchisement and the gutting of the Racial Justice Act, all of which have clear racial

---

[27] I will leave an in-depth discussion of that for another book, but I highly recommend Training for Change as a resource, and particularly Daniel Hunter's work. www.trainingforchange.org/

connotations. In the subtle political landscape of the South, some might have found it easy to dismiss my courageous Black colleagues as playing some kind of racial politics in their opposition to these misguided policies. It was slightly harder to do that because Rob Stephens, a young White man who worked for the NAACP at the time, and I were there. This wasn't just a 'Black issue.' It was a justice issue.

I don't want to exaggerate the significance of that contribution. Rob and I were followers in that group, not leaders. Rev. Barber mentioned our diversity as something that was good about our group, though, and I'm glad we could provide it. Identity should never be a basis for one person to be valued more highly than another, but it is unwise to neglect its strategic significance and the particular tools it offers. It also can be helpful in determining what is specifically ours to do.

In my case, I was also keenly aware that I have an audience as a musician, many of whom would be surprised to find that I had been arrested and would want to know why. That was precisely our goal, to get the word out about some terrible things that were going on in the legislature. To give people a reason to pay attention and learn for themselves what was happening. When I added those things up, this seemed like it was mine to do.

Sometimes, our callings sneak up on us. Abby Goldberg struggled for some time to come up with a seventh-grade school project, until one day, she says, the idea flew in her face—literally: a plastic bag from a nearby garbage dump blew up on a windy day and ran right into her. She started to investigate one-use plastic shopping bags, and became increasingly disturbed by what she found. As an animal lover, she recoiled at images of sea animals tangled in them. Doing her own field research, she counted 173 bags leaving just one checkout aisle in her local grocery store in a two-hour period. Abby had a great idea for her school project: she would get her town to ban plastic bags.

When her research led her to discover a bill moving through her state legislature, though, she got really mad. The bill would *ban* municipalities from *banning* plastic bags, while requiring them to meet very low standards of recycled content in those bags, thus enabling them to pitch the bill as an environmental initiative, deceptively calling it the 'Plastic Bag and Film Recycling Act'.

Abby's response was not what you might expect from a twelve-year-old. She started an online petition to the governor asking him to veto the bill when it reached his desk. More than 174,000 people signed that petition, myself included. The petition got significant press coverage, and as more people learned what was in the bill, public opposition naturally grew.

The governor called Abby at home one night, just as she was going to sleep, to tell her that he had decided to veto the bill, and to thank her. Not bad for a seventh grader.

Abby's story is extremely compelling, and she would be an impressive young woman regardless of her age, but her youth is a significant part of this story. When I asked her what effect her age has had on her activism, she said, "I tell other kids to use being a kid to their advantage. We know a lot about social media, we have lots of friends, and we have time to get involved. Actually I think it is our job to tell the adults about problems in the world. Sometimes adults are too busy to see all the problems."

On the other end of the age spectrum, we find the Raging Grannies, who are often found at various protests singing well-known melodies with brand new, self-penned words with great passion and conviction. They are a group of older women, and most of them really are grandmothers. Their activism seems somewhat surprising because they don't fit our stereotypes of what activists look like. They make headlines both because they are adorable and because they are surprising, thereby getting the word out about the important things they stand for, and sometimes against.

I co-billed with a group of Raging Grannies at a peace conference in Berlin on the third anniversary of the launch of the Iraq war. I was invited to speak to German peace activists because I was a peace activist in the U.S. The Europeans I met on that trip were not seeing anything in their media about a peace movement in the United States, so they were amazed to learn that there was one. In that case, my nationality was significant. They needed to know that there were dissenting voices here in the United States.

Closer to home, my father was arrested in the Moral Mondays movement here in North Carolina the week after I was. At that time, he was an eighty-one-year-old retired Presbyterian pastor, well-respected and dignified, with no previous history of civil disobedience. He felt compelled by his faith to take that stand due to Biblical teachings about defending and caring for the poor, who are currently under assault by our state government. I wrote a blog about his arrest called *Taking My Dad to Jail for Father's Day*, and it was very widely read. Lots of people know retired ministers; very few of us expect them to get arrested. Because of who he is, my dad's story resonated with a lot of people.

As I write this, my eyes wander up to the bookshelf in my friends' beautiful cabin where I am writing, and they fall on Bell Hooks' book *Ain't I a Woman*. It is titled after Sojourner Truth's famed speech in 1852, where, as Hooks puts it, she "became one of the first feminists to call their attention to the lot of the female black slave woman who, compelled by circumstance to labor alongside black men, was a living embodiment of the truth that women could be the world-equals of men." She was a 'living embodiment' of the story she told. Her identity was fundamental to her ideas and her efficacy in sharing them so persuasively.

My friend Allyson Caison lives in Johnston County, North Carolina. Sitting around a Boy Scout campfire in the late nineties, she first learned of a company called Aero Contractors, which flew 'extraordinary rendition' flights for the CIA from her local rural airport.

From Johnston County, planes flew all over the world, nabbing terror suspects, chaining them to the floor, and flying them to countries where they could be tortured and interrogated without any legal process or charges being filed.[28] Allyson did not think this was right, and she was deeply troubled that these flights were based right in her own backyard.

As she probed further into this, she was dismayed to

---

[28] For more on this, read Ghost Plane by Stephen Grey.

discover that two of the principal players at Aero were parents of her children's friends. She knew them well.

Allyson is a real estate agent, and it would have been reasonable for her to demure, thinking that stirring the political pot in her small town could ruin her business. But she had a sense of moral obligation. It was not only her country doing this, it was her own town. In fact, it was people she knew.

Allyson got involved with an organization called North Carolina Stop Torture Now, which is led by a courageous and knowledgeable woman named Christina Cowger. They organized a small vigil in October of 2007, and Allyson was in charge of acquiring permits. There were plenty of hoops to jump through, and she encountered open hostility and resistance among some of the town's leadership. It was an extremely stressful time for her. In the end, though, they held the event.

That early vigil led to further actions and protests, and over the years, the issue has moved further into the mainstream. Allyson, Christina, and others have appeared before the County Commissioners on many, many occasions, expressing their concerns. At one such meeting, Allyson read an entire letter by Anna Britel, the wife of rendition and torture survivor Kassim Britel. She told me that she broke out in hives from anxiety, but she still read the letter. She needed them to understand the humanity of the victims. It has been a long, slow process, as effective activism usually is, but ultimately, it is working.

The way Allyson puts it, "When you first start filling a bucket one drop at a time, for a long time you can't even perceive that the bucket has any drops (it's a big bucket). But eventually, one small drop at a time, it fills up and goes over the top. So each small act of kindness on behalf of the world's most vulnerable adds to the great bucket. And we will tip to goodness—I believe that with my whole heart."

By the way, it seems important to note that Allyson was voted realtor of the year in 2013 by the Johnston County Realtors Association. Apparently her activism has not damaged the respect her peers have for her or her business.

As you consider what you are called to do in the world, it may be useful to consider what role your identity might play in your contributions. There may be roadsigns in the answers to these questions: Who are you? Where are you from? Who do you represent? How do others see you? What do you care about that people might not expect you to care about? What do you bring because of who you are?

CHAPTER EIGHTEEN

The Not-So-Radical Activist

*We cannot do everything, and there is a sense
of liberation in realizing that. This enables us
to do something, and to do it very well.*

— Bishop Ken Untener, The Prayer of Oscar Romero

Earlier in this book you read about Jo Ann Robinson, who, along with two of her students, stayed up all night after Rosa Parks was arrested, making copies of a bus boycott flier to be distributed around Montgomery. Robinson's book, *The Montgomery Bus Boycott and the Women Who Started It*, goes on to describe a meeting the next day with the principal of the college where she taught, Alabama State University.

After she finished teaching an 8AM class, she left with the two students to deposit the fliers at designated drop points, where members and friends of the Women's Political Council would pick them up and distribute them further.

But when she returned to campus to teach her 2 o'clock class, she found a note from Dr. H. Councill Trenholm, the president of the college, asking her to come to his office immediately. Another teacher had brought a copy of the flier to President Trenholm, and Robinson writes that when she entered his office, he was, "very angry and visibly shaken." He told her that he had sent another teacher to cover her class, and he demanded an explanation.

Ms. Robinson's book clearly demonstrates her deep respect for President Trenholm. He had taken over when the school was a tiny junior college and, through deep investment of time, effort, and sometimes even his own money, had grown it into a successful senior college with a large and growing enrollment. He had engaged with the community, offering scholarships to needy and promising prospective students and earning the trust and investment of business people.

During that meeting, Robinson writes, she was aware that she might lose her job, but was willing to do so. She informed President Trenholm of Rosa Parks' arrest and the earlier incarceration of Claudette Colvin, a local teenager, under similar circumstances. She described the outrageous and frequent ill treatment of Black women and men on the public buses. She told him that she had calculated the costs of the paper they had used for the fliers, and that the Women's Political Council would reimburse the school in full. (Actually, the WPC had no treasury. She payed that bill personally.)

He stopped her frequently and asked further questions. Robinson noticed that, "As I talked, I could see the anger slowly receding from his face and heard his tone of voice softening."

When he had asked all that he needed to and she had answered, they both sat quietly for a time. At the end of that silence, although Robinson writes that, "He seemed to have aged years in the brief span of our conversation," Trenholm finally spoke, "Your group must continue to press for civil rights."

He also cautioned her, however, not to neglect her responsibilities as a faculty member, to be careful to stay out of the limelight, and not to involve the college in the movement.

It would be easy to cast that last speech as pretty lukewarm, or even an Uncle Tom complicity. While people all over Montgomery were ramping up to engage in this boycott, which could be extremely dangerous for them, Dr. Trenholm's response was to ask Jo Ann Robinson to be less visible and to make sure she didn't involve the college? People were risking violence and loss of jobs (and therefore family income), and he was worried about his school's reputation?

That's not how Jo Ann Robinson saw it, though, and she offers this further information:

Dr. Trenholm did not participate personally in the boycott, but he was mentally and spiritually involved—and deeply so! He was financially involved, too, and often contributed to the collections for people who were suffering because of the loss of their jobs...

...As we will see, once the battle was begun, the bus company and city officials would request Dr. Trenholm to sit on a board with them to help arrive at a satisfactory conclusion of the boycott.

Providing a sympathetic voice at the table in those negotiations was certainly an important role to play, and Dr. Trenholm could not have done it if he had lost his position at the college due to being too publicly radical. Likewise, he could not have provided the desperately needed financial support he did if he were out of work. He needed to be a moderate voice publicly in order to support the cause in significant ways that no one else could offer.

There is often an unspoken assumption that the most radical and outspoken activists are the most deeply committed and important for a cause, but I don't think history bears that out.

This story, like all stories, is open to interpretation. Was this a hypocritical cop-out or the strategic wisdom of a committed supporter who rightly perceived his particular role and contribution?

It seems to me that there is often an unspoken assumption that the most radical and outspoken activists are the most deeply committed and important for a cause, but I don't think history bears that out.

My friend and mentor Dan Buttry, whose actual job title is 'Global Consultant for Peace', introduced me to a tool called the Spectrum of Allies, also used by Training for Change in their workshops.

The Spectrum of Allies is a tool for considering a possible action and what effect it might have, looking at whether it is more likely to help achieve your goals or backfire. It plots all of the stakeholders in a given conflict along a graph, categorizing them as 1) active allies, 2) passive allies, 3) neutral, 4) passive opponents, or 5) active opponents.[29]

To shift the trajectory of a large group—like a nation, for instance—a whole lot of people need to move a little bit. The ideal action would turn your active opponents into passive opponents, your passive opponents neutral, some neutral people into passive allies and some passive allies into active allies, though in the real world one action seldom has that entire effect. In an election or similar voting context, it is really just the shift in the middle of the spectrum that usually results in a policy change, but in terms of large societal transformations, each of those shifts counts for a great deal. It is possible, though extremely rare, for someone to move in one dramatic shift from active opponent to active ally, but that kind of radical shift is not necessary. Every little move matters, from any of those categories into the one next to it.

This is what happened when Rosa Parks was arrested. As a nation, we saw this dignified, non-threatening woman arrested for refusing to give up a seat that she had paid for, simply because of her skin color. This clear injustice caused some people who had been passively sympathetic to the cause of racial equality to get involved and take action, some people who had simply accepted the status quo as 'the way things are' to become passively sympathetic to the protestors, some who

_____

[29] Training for Change is a non-profit organization that spreads the skills of democratic, nonviolent social change. I highly recommend their trainings and tools. http://www.trainingforchange.org/

had been passively supportive of segregation and inequality to question themselves and move toward neutrality. Perhaps it even led some who had been actively involved in oppression to become less active.

I don't want to oversimplify the story. There were doubtless others who had been passively opposed to the aims of the boycotters who became more active in their opposition as they saw their privilege threatened. When injustice is challenged, some sort of backlash is almost inevitable. On the whole, though, this action shook people from their assumptions and caused them to reevaluate. Through this and other actions, the nation gradually perceived the everyday injustice in which we were participating, became increasingly uncomfortable with it, and shifted our sympathies.

This perspective further challenges the assumption above that more dramatic and radical acts and actors count more. If large scale change requires subtle shifts all along the spectrum, then the most outspoken activists are *not* necessarily the most important or effective in a movement. On their own, all the way to one side of the spectrum, they simply can't get much done. If their rhetoric and tactics are too shocking to the mainstream, they don't recruit anyone beyond the people in their immediate proximity on that graph.

Activists who are deep into a movement for a particular cause sometimes forget this and dismiss the small efforts and sympathies of people who are, in fact, our allies—or could be, if we would offer them a path. Worse yet, we sometimes impose these litmus test judgments on our own efforts, feeling ineffectual or weak because, for instance, we don't have bold bumper stickers on our cars, or haven't marched in the streets, or haven't been to jail.

Sometimes a bumper sticker can provoke a good conversation, but sometimes it can prevent one. Sometimes marching in the streets is extremely important, but it may be that it is not your way to contribute. Sometimes civil disobedience is good strategy, sometimes it is merely self-congratulatory, a personal struggle rather than a public service.

Because large changes require small shifts all along the spectrum, however, we mustn't dismiss our own small efforts, or those of the people around us. It's not just that they matter; they are often essential. Once more, the question is not, 'Am I doing enough?' but rather, 'Am I doing what is mine to do?'

So what *is* yours to do? It's time to turn our attention to that question and to a series of smaller questions that may help lead us to its answers.

Pick One

Pick One

*One cannot level one's moral lance at every evil
in the universe. There are just too many of them.
But you can do something, and the difference
between doing something and doing nothing
is everything.*

— Daniel Berrigan

Having established that big changes are made up of small ones, that normal people change things, not heroes, that effective activism can take many forms (including not-so-radical ones), that real change is made by imperfect people, that hope and love are choices rather than circumstances, that worldchanging requires creativity, (and there are often more options than the options we can see), that our own gifts may have as much to do with our callings as the condition of the world around us, that we have many callings, not just one big one... having established all that, there's one more question to ask.

What will you do about it?

This last section of this book walks you through some simple questions in an effort to help you determine what may be calling to you next. We have spaced them out so that you can flip the page and answer each in turn. I think this works best if you don't look ahead but answer each one before moving on to the next.

The most important thing to remember in this exercise is that we are not trying to discern your Calling with a big 'C'. This is not intended to help you figure out what to do with your *Life*, only what you're supposed to work on *next*.

With that in mind, I suggest that you write down the very first thing that comes to your mind in response to each of these questions. Don't think about it. Don't look for your *best* answer, just give your *first* answer. You can always go back and do it again.

If you prefer to do this digitally, you can go to PickOne.org, which will ask you the same questions and give you a chance to share your answers with others if you like (or keep them private if you don't, but commit to yourself and get a reminder email later to see how it's going). You can also read what others are up to, which you may find inspiring.

Ready? Get a pen, then turn the page!

Care:
What matters to you?

What is driving you nuts?

Put otherwise, what is it, on any scale from family to planetary, that you just can't believe people are allowing to happen? What doesn't seem right to you?

Or, if you would rather answer this question, what really excites you? What are people doing that really makes you sit up straighter and believe in humanity?

Just your first thought, not your best answer.

Contribute:
What do you bring that not everyone can bring?

What do you love doing? What are you good at?

Both questions are important to consider, as unrelated to worldchanging as they may seem.

This is not a time for humility, at least in the misguided, commonly understood sense of refusing to acknowledge your strengths. Be honest with yourself.

What are your gifts?

Connect:

Where can you find a community of people who are also concerned about the thing you care about?

Community matters, and we generally come up with better ideas when we work them out in groups. Certainly we have larger impact when we motivate each other and work together. Remember, it's movements that make big changes.

Where are your people?

Choose:
What is one small thing you can do this week?

How can you step toward this thing you care about in some small way? What's one small thing you can do right now, or at the latest, this week?

Note that I said *small* (perhaps I should write SMALL in great big letters, with full irony intended). This isn't about being a hero. It's about getting started and moving in the right direction.

Commit:
Write it down, then do that thing.

Really.

Write it on a piece of paper right now and put that piece of paper on your bathroom mirror, or in your pocket, or on your dashboard, or in your purse, or wherever it is going to annoy you until you get it done.

When you actually do it, you can put that piece of paper on your fridge in celebration, or burn it with a prayer of thanksgiving, or just recycle it. You can also go to PickOne.org and answer these questions there.

Rinse and Repeat:

Yeah, I know. That's not a question (and it doesn't even start with 'C'!).

Taking that first step is wonderful and huge. You've just changed from being passive to being an active-ist. You're engaging with something you care about, and this is, in fact, how the world changes.

This is not the end of the story, however; it's the beginning. When you're done, there are a few more questions that come up. What did you learn from that experience? What will you do now? Does your experience call you further in to commitment to that issue, or are you feeling pulled elsewhere? As soon as you're ready, go back to question one and do it again.

Blessings on the journey that unfolds.

About PickOne.org

In the last few months, I have had a lot of conversations with good friends, colleagues, and mentors about this book and the ideas that fill it—and about another related idea.

My friends Murphy and Kenny own a company called Kudzu Branding Co. here in Black Mountain, North Carolina. They're good buddies of ours. My wife and Murphy went to high school together back in the day, and Kenny and I have known each other for almost as long. They are smart and creative people, and they have given me great ideas about how to communicate and raise awareness around things I care about.

Not long ago, Murphy came up with the idea of printing "Pick One" on some guitar picks and using it as a kind of slogan. To me, that means this: don't be overwhelmed, just pick one thing you want to work on, then pick one thing you can do about it. I like it.

Then we had the idea of creating a web site where people could share their passions (what they care about), and their commitments (what they intend to do about it). Seemed like a natural next step, a place where people could inspire each other, connect and possibly even spark a movement.

So we checked to see if PickOne.org was available. Someone owned it, we found, but there was no web site there. Kenny found the owner, wrote to him in the U.K., and asked if the site was for sale. He wrote back pleasantly and said that it was for sale, and that he was asking $17,000.

That's probably not an unreasonable asking price for a web address that is also such a common phrase, but it's a bit out of this folksinger's budget. Kenny shared the response with me and asked what he should say.

I told Kenny that I could offer $800 or so, and maybe could even bargain up to $1200 if the man who owned the URL stopped laughing long enough to write back.

Happily, however, Kenny is smarter than I am. Instead of doing what I asked him to do, he responded to the owner of the site and told him what we wanted to do with it.

The owner of the site replied and said that he would like to *give the site to us*. Apparently he had an idea to do something similar but was excited that we were actually going to get it off the ground, and he wanted to support that.

Quite a story for the launch of this particular web site, isn't it? Here is a man contributing what only he can, doing the thing that is his to do, and potentially influencing many others. Beautiful, and poetically self-illustrating.

The web site asks the questions in this chapter and gives you a chance to share your answers, inspire others, and check out what they are doing so that you can be inspired as well. It will even send you a quick follow-up email a little while later to see how things are going.

Thank you for taking the time to read this book. And what's more, thank you for being the kind of person who cares about the influence you're having in the world. If you were not that kind of person, you would not have read it. So thank you.

Now go change the world.

About Homeless Fonts

The inset quotes, or 'pull quotes', in this book are in a font called 'Guillermo', which can be purchased at homelessfonts.org. The font is based on the handwriting of a man named Guillermo, who lives in Barcelona, Spain. Homelessfonts is an initiative of the Arrels Foundation, which is creating fonts in partnership with homeless people in Barcelona, using the same unique handwriting that they use to make themselves visible on the street.

This font and several others can be purchased at homelessfonts.org.

Endnotes

Preface

p. xi **"In their book *The Dragonfly Effect...*"**
Smith, Andy, and Jennifer Lynnm Aaker. *The Dragonfly Effect.*
San Francisco: Jossey-Bass, 2010.

p. xiv **"As Alexia Salvatierra and Peter Heitzel point out in their book *Faith-Rooted Organizing...*"**
Salvatierra, Alexia, and Peter Heitzel. *Faith-Rooted Organizing: Mobilizing the Church in Service to the World.*
Downers Grove: InterVarsity Press, 2014. p. 88

Chapter 1: Changing My World

p. 26 **"Historian Howard Zinn argues..."**
Zinn, Howard. *A People's History of the United States.*
New York, NY: HarperCollins Publishers, 2005. p. 8.

Chapter 2: What Are You Talking About?

p. 27 **"The German philosopher Johann Georg Hamann..."**
Koestler, Arthur. *The Act of Creation.*
New York: Penguin Books, 1990. p. 173.

p. 28 **"'Hope is not prognostication...'"**
Havel, Václav. *Disturbing the Peace.* Translated by Paul Wilson.
New York, NY: Vintage Books, [1986] 1991. p. 181.
"The historian Howard Zinn writes..."
Zinn, Howard. *A Power Governments Cannot Suppress.*
San Francisco, CA: City Lights Publishers, 2006. p. 270.

p. 33 **"In his 2012 book *Across that Bridge,* Lewis described..."**
Lewis, John. Across that Bridge. Hyperion: New York, NY, 2012. p. 153

Chapter 4: Out of the Blue

p. 60 **"...John Lewis did not start out being beaten into a coma on the Edmund Pettus bridge...."**
Lewis, John. *Walking with the Wind.* New York, NY: Harvest Books, 1999. p. 75-87.

Chapter 5: Heroes and Movements

p. 68   **"Paul Loeb articulates this well in his bestseller *Soul of a Citizen...*"**
Loeb, Paul. *Soul of a Citizen.* New York: St. Martin's Press, 1999. p. 34.

p. 69   **"...famed Catholic Worker activist Dorothy Day, who said of her self and her fellow workers..."**
Van Biema, David. "Rhythm of the Saints: Candidate Saints: Dorothy Day." *Time Magazine.*
http://content.time.com/time/specials/packages/article/
0,28804,1850894_1850895_1850863,00.html
"In an interview with the *New York Times*, Wesley Autry said..."
Buckley, Cara. "Man Is Rescued by Stranger on Subway Tracks."
The New York Times, January 3, 2007.
"In George W. Bush's 2007 State of the Union Address..."
The White House. President Bush Delivers State of the Union Address."
January 23, 2007.
http://georgewbush-whitehouse.archives.gov/news/releases/2007/
01/20070123-2.html

p. 72   **"It was called 'The 8 Most Overrated People in History'..."**
Juddery, Mark. "The 8 Most Overrated People in History."
The Huffington Post, August 21, 2010.
http://www.huffingtonpost.com/mark-juddery/overrated
people_b_688237.html#s129491&title=Mahatma_Gandhi

p. 74   **"Rosa Parks seemed to agree..."**
Brook, Tom Vanden. "Parks courage changed nation."
USA Today, October 25, 2005.
http://usatoday30.usatoday.com/news/nation/2005-10-24-parks-
detailedobit_x.htm

p. 75   **"Just between the years of 2000 and 2006, organized non-violent civilian movements successfully challenged entrenched power..."**
Stephan, Maria J., and Erica Chenoweth. "Why Civil Resistance Works." *International Security* 33.1 (2008): 7-44. doi: 10.1162/isec. 2008.33.1.7.
"Étienne de la Boétie, a young 16th-century political theorist..."
de la Boétie, Étienne. *The Discourse of Voluntary Servitude.*
Translated by Harry Kurz. Indianapolis: Liberty Fund, Inc., [1576] 2014.
http://oll.libertyfund.org/pages/etienne-de-la-boetie-discourse-of-
voluntary-servitude-1576.

p.76   **"And movements don't need lots of leaders; they need lots of participants..."** One of my favorite illustrations of this concept is a video by Derek Sivers: http://sivers.org/ff

Chapter 6: Small Change

p. 77   **"...as Rosa Parks wrote in her autobiography..."**
Parks, Rosa. *My Story.* New York: Puffin Books, 1992. p. 136.

p. 78   **"'I was the only woman there...'"**
Parks, Rosa. *My Story.* New York: Puffin Books, 1992. pp. 80-81.

p. 82   **"...one of my favorites is the story of Jo Ann Robinson..."**
Robinson, Jo Ann Gibson. *The Montgomery Bus Boycott and the Women Who Started It.*
Knoxville: The University of Tennessee Press, 1987, pp. 50-54.

Chapter 7: The Flawed Hero

p. 90   **"Aleksandr Solzhenitsyn got it right when he said..."**
Solzhenitsyn, Aleksandr. *The Gulag Archipelago 1918-56.*
Translated by Thomas P. Whitney. New York: Harper & Row, 1973.

Chapter 8: Paved with Good Intentions

p. 93-94 **"Healthcare activist, doctor, and author Paul Farmer has said..."**
Farmer, Paul. "Partner's in Health Website." http://www.pih.org/.

p. 96   **"The recent books Toxic Charity and When Helping Hurts..."**
Lupton, Robert D. *Toxic Charity.* New York: HarperOne, 2012.
Corbett, Steve, and Brian Fikkert. *When Helping Hurts.*
Chicago: Moody Publishers, 2012.

Chapter 9: Community

p. 101 **"As clown activist Patch Adams writes in his book House Calls..."**
Adams, Patch, M.D. *House Calls: How We Can All Heal the World One Visit at a Time.* San Francisco: Robert D. Reed Publishers, 1998. p. 44.

p. 102 **"As sociologist John Brueggemann writes in his book *Rich, Free, and Miserable...*"** Brueggemann, John. *Rich, Free, and Miserable.*
New York: Rowman and Littlefield Publishers, 2012. p. 105

p. 103 **"In the months following the 9/11 attacks, my friend Lyndon Harris..."**
For more on that story, I recommend Krystyna Sanderson's photo book, *Light at Ground Zero* (Square Halo Books, 2004).

p. 110 **"As Roger Fisher and William Ury write in their small and seminal book *Getting to Yes...*"** Fisher, Roger, and William Ury.
Getting to Yes: Negotiating Agreement Without Giving In.
New York: Penguin Books, 1983. p. 42

p. 113 **"In their insightful book Switch: How to Change Things When Change Is Hard..."** Heath, Chip, and Dan Heath. *Switch: How to Change Things When Change Is Hard.* New York: Broadway Books, 2010. p. 222.

p. 119 **"... dramatic stories told by Rev. Barber and Rev. Kojo Nantambu, who was around when the Wilmington Ten were arrested."** For more on the Wilmington Ten, see: http://www2.lib.unc.edu/ncc/ref/nchistory/feb2005/

Chapter 10: Creativity and Worldchanging

p. 125 **"On May 26, 2007, the Ku Klux Klan gathered for a rally in Knoxville, Tennessee...."** Santoso, Alex. "Clowns Kicked KKK Asses." *Neatorama*, September 3, 2007. http://www.neatorama.com/2007/09/03/clowns-kicked-kkk-asses/#!bn4liE **"The problem with the first approach is that, in the words of Dr. King..."** King, Martin Luther Jr. "Loving Your Enemies." *Strength to Love.* Minneapolis: Fortress Press, [1963] 2010. p. 47.

p. 126 **"...Martin Luther King, Jr. wrote in his famous 'Letter from a Birmingham Jail.'"** King, Martin Luther Jr. "Letter from a Birmingham Jail." April 16, 1963. Philadelphia: University of Pennsylvania African Studies Center. http://www.africa.upenn.edu/Articles_Gen/Letter_Birmingham.html

p. 128 **"As John Lewis wrote in his book *Across that Bridge...*"** Lewis, John. Across that Bridge. Hyperion: New York, NY, 2012. p. 136. **"Artist Peter von Tiesenhausen was being threatened by oil corporations..."** "Opposition to Drilling Elevated to an Art Form." *The Edmonton Journal,* February 27, 2006. http://www.canada.com/story_print.html?id=a271ed7f-d512-4a26-9b32-226ba7bfb1ea&sponsor=

p. 129 **"Julia Cameron, in her classic book on creativity, *The Artist's Way*, writes..."** Cameron, Julia. The Artist's Way. New York: Tarcher/Putnam, 1992. p. 3.

p. 132 **"Rosa Parks, at the end of her autobiography...wrote with wonder..."** Parks, Rosa. *My Story.* New York: Puffin Books, 1992. p. 186.

p. 134 **"Thoreau describes these two steps to creation..."** Thoreau, Henry David. *Walden.* New York: Bantam Books, [1854] 1989. p. 343. **"Emily Dickinson said it another way..."** Grabher, Gurdun, Roland Hagenbuchle, and Cristanne Miller, eds.

The Emily Dickinson Handbook. Amherst: University of
Massachusetts Press, 1998. p. 282.

**"The respected conflict transformation theorist and practitioner
John Paul Lederach..."**
Lederach, John Paul. *The Moral Imagination.*
Oxford: Oxford University Press, 2005. p. 69.

p. 135 **"The famed Russian actor and theater director Konstantin
Sergeievich Stanislavski..."**
White, R. Andrew, ed. *The Routledge Companion to Stanislovsky.*
New York: Routledge, 2014.

"Kim Rosen, the author of *Saved By a Poem*...writes that..."
Rosen, Kim. "Where Words Melt Walls: The Peacemaking Power
of Poetry." *The Huffington Post*, June 21, 2010.
http://www.huffingtonpost.com/kim-rosen/where-words-melt-walls-
th_b_615133.html

p. 136 **"In another effort to approach a serious topic through art, I put the
story of the clowns and the Klan to rhyme..."**
Find out more about the book, *White Flour* (2012) at
www.whiteflourbook.com

p. 137 **"In November of 2012, there was a neo-Nazi rally in
Charlotte, NC..."**
Manual-Logan, Ruth. "KKK Protestors Clowned by Counter-Protest,
Outnumbered 5 to 1." News One, November 13, 2012.
http://newsone.com/2081264/kkk-charlotte-nc/

Chapter 11: Stumbling Toward Light

p. 151 **"In her fascinating Book *Being Wrong*, Kathryn Schulz
writes..."**
Schulz, Kathryn. *Being Wrong: Adventures in the Margin of Error.*
New York: HarperCollins, 2010.

Chapter 13: What's Most Important?

p. 160 **"...given that the average person in the U.S. now has several
careers over the course of their lives."**
Morrison, Robert F., and Jerome Adams.
Contemporary Career Development Issues.
Hillsdale: Lawrence Erblaum Associates, 1991. p. 80.

p. 163 **"Noam Chomsky, the famous linguist and activist, talking
with Bill Moyers..."**
Moyers, Bill. *A World of Ideas.* New York: Doubleday, 1989. p. 56.

"'Compassion fatigue' is a concept that was introduced..."
"Self-Study Unit 3: Photography and Trauma."
The Dart Center for Journalism and Trauma.
Columbia University Graduate School of Journalism.
http://dartcenter.org/content/self-study-unit-3-photography-
trauma-3#.U9Y6d4BdWGl

Chapter 15: What Do You Bring?

p. 173   **"Howard Thurman, an author, philosopher, and preacher who was**
         a mentor to Martin Luther King, Jr., said..."
         Bailie, Gil. *Violence Unveiled.*
         New York: Crossroad Publishing Company, 1996. p. xv.
p. 174   **"'Faith contains a certain ferocity...'"**
         LeVoy, Gregg Michael. *Callings: Finding and Following an Authentic Life.*
         New York: Three Rivers Press, 1997. p. 265.
p. 180   **"In the last few pages of Rosa Parks' autobiography..."**
         Parks, Rosa. *My Story.* New York: Puffin Books, 1992. p. 180.

Chapter 17: The Power In Who You Are

p. 189   **"Ivo Markovic, the founder of the choir, tells the story of its**
         origins..."
         Conrad, Keziah. "Ivo Markovich." *The Beyond Intractability Project.*
         Boulder: Conflict Information Consortium of the University of
         Colorado, March 2007.
         http://www.beyondintractability.org/profile/ivo-markovic.
         "In an article about Pontanima, Andrew Packman writes..."
         Packman, Andrew. "Interfaith Repertoire: A Bosnian Choir Sings
         Reconciliation." *The Christian Century*, June 13. 2012.
p. 198   **"...they fall on Bell Hooks' book *Ain't I a Woman.*"**
         Hooks, Bell. *Ain't I a Woman: Black Women and Feminism.*
         New York: South End Press, 1981. p. 159-160.

Chapter 18: The Not-So-Radical Activist

p. 201   **"Robinson writes that when she entered his office..."**
         Robinson, Jo Ann Gibson.
         The Montgomery Bus Boycott and the Women Who Started It.
         Knoxville: The University of Tennessee Press, 1987. p. 48ff.
p. 203   **"'Dr. Trenholm did not participate personally in the boycott...'"**
         Robinson, Jo Ann Gibson.
         The Montgomery Bus Boycott and the Women Who Started It.
         Knoxville: The University of Tennessee Press, 1987. p. 50.

Notes

Notes

Notes

Notes

Notes